COSMOS & HEARTH

The publication of this book was assisted by a bequest from Josiah H. Chase to honor his parents, Ellen Rankin Chase and Josiah Hook Chase, Minnesota territorial pioneers.

COSMOS & HEARTH

a cosmopolite's viewpoint

YI-FU TUAN

University of Minnesota Press

Minneapolis

London

Published by the University of Minnesota Press
111 Third Avenue South, Suite 290, Minneapolis, MN 55401-2520
Printed in the United States of America on acid-free paper

Library of Congress Cataloging-in-Publication Data

Tuan, Yi-fu, 1930-
    Cosmos and hearth : a cosmopolite's viewpoint / Yi-fu Tuan.
        p.   cm.
    Includes index.
    ISBN 0-8166-2730-4 (hc)
    1. Tuan, Yi-fu, 1930-   2. Chinese Americans—Biography.   3. United
States—Civilization.   4. China—Civilization.   5. Comparative
civilization.   6. Internationalism.   I. Title.
E184.C5T84   1996
973'.04951—dc20   95-41240

The University of Minnesota is an
equal-opportunity educator and employer.

To PWP

CONTENTS

ACKNOWLEDGMENTS

I would like to acknowledge intellectual stimulation and help from the following scholars and colleagues: Merle Curti, Edward Friedman, Martin Lewis, Chun-jo Liu, Sharon Ruch, Robert Sack, Donald K. Smith, and S. T. Wong. They are, of course, in no way responsible for those errors of fact and interpretation that remain. The book, though rooted in my personal experience of two cultures, has its immediate genesis in a geography seminar titled "Cosmopolitanism and Place." It gives me pleasure to thank all the students who participated and, especially, Valentin Bogorov, Steven Hoelscher, Eric Olmanson, and Karen Till, who continue to offer me advice and encouragement. Finally, if the reader is a little put off by the book's undertone of optimism, blame should be laid on two geography departments—Minnesota and Wisconsin. After twenty-five years of working in an environment of unstinting support and collegiality, how can I not be somewhat influenced?

TWO SCALES AND AUTOBIOGRAPHY

In *The Wind in the Willows*, Mole has just returned to his cozy home underground. Soon he lays his head contentedly on his pillow. Before he closes his eyes he lets them wander around his room, "mellow in the glow of the firelight . . . on familiar friendly things." How good it is to be back! Yet he would not want to abandon the splendid spaces above ground; he has no intention of turning his back on sun and air and creeping home and staying there. "The upper world was too strong, it called to him still, even down there, and he knew he must return to the larger stage."[1]

To what degree do we at the end of the twentieth century share Mole's sentiment? Isn't there for many of us a strong urge to stay in our burrow, to find sustenance there in the familiar things rather than on "the larger stage" of sun and air, which can seem somewhat repellent—the sun not warming but blistering and desiccating, the air not vivifying but chilling? Even in the United States, which once acclaimed mobility and space, "place" now seems the favored word, and in the world generally, cultural particularism and ethnic heritage carry greater resonance—arouse more positive feelings—than cosmopolitanism and universalism, programs that, from the Enlightenment to much of the first part of the twentieth century, commanded emotional and intellectual allegiance among leaders of opinion.

At a basic (reflex) level, the shift is surprising if only because the life-path of a human being moves naturally from "home" to "world," from "hearth" to "cosmos." We grow into a larger world. Not to do so is to lead a stunted life. In all human cultures, one's stages of maturation are celebrated, because at each stage one enters a larger sphere of activity and responsibility. The judgment against patriarchal societies is that in them women are made to stay at the hearth. The judgment against hierarchical societies is that there members of the lower class are confined to a domestic work sphere (home, village, neighborhood) while the elite move on to enjoy the world. The elite can have both world *and* home; they can be cosmopolitan and yet return to the hearth for nurturance and renewal. They are privileged. Enlightened societies seek to extend the privilege to more and more people who formerly suffered constraint so that a time will come when none need feel that the edge of their home is the edge of their world.

Nevertheless, like Mole, many human beings may well feel a certain ambivalence toward both ends of the geographic scale. Hearth, though nurturing, can be too confining; cosmos, though liberating, can be bewildering and threatening. In small preliterate communities, adulthood is unambiguously preferred to earlier stages of life. Nostalgia for the small world of childhood is practically unknown, perhaps because the adult world, though much larger, is nonthreatening, being fairly stable: once young adults have submitted to an initiation rite and learned the basic social and technical skills of their group, they are assured of certain privileges that they can expect to retain without further struggle. In complex literate societies, life in the public sphere is more open, less certain; and in modern societies, it is far more open, far less certain still.

Let China and the United States, as complex societies, illustrate the differences. In traditional China, the scholar-gentry elite arrogate to themselves the cosmos—both the sacred one of ceremonies and rituals and the secular one of worldly goods and privileges. Climbing the ladder of success has, however, never been easy even for the privileged: China's history is full of the rise and fall of great families. The very fact that the large social world is open makes for a certain anxiousness, a lack of lasting contentment. Homesickness is a common theme in Chinese poetry, conditioned in part by the custom of assigning officials to posts distant from their hometowns: magistrates can anticipate the pain of uprooting even as they rejoice in the news of promotion to preside over a larger city.[2] Compared with the privileged, the ambition of ordinary people has little scope: their move up in the world can seldom be more than a small step. As compensation, they retain their sense of social and cultural ease.

In one sphere of life, however, the Chinese elite undoubtedly feel more secure—the sphere of nature. Civilization's material achievements promote that assurance: high officials in particular can see how human ingenuity and power have built extensive irrigation and flood-control works that counter nature's potential for devastation. Cosmic rites, marking in a dignified way the motion of the heavenly bodies and the swing of the seasons, are themselves a sign of this confidence. To the gentry and scholar-officials, the cosmos is awe-inspiring without being awe-full; its many mysteries notwithstanding, it is essentially impersonal, harmonious, and accessible to human reason. By contrast, to peasant farmers who make up the bulk of the population, nature is both fearsome and unpredictable, to be propitiated or forfended by sacrifice and magic. The peasant's homeplace, reassuring in its familiarity and timeless ways, is yet haunted by spirits and demons, the existence of which is a sure sign of their livelihood's intractable dysfunctions and insecurity. Thus, both "home" (hearth) and "world" (cosmos) have their advantages and disadvantages. Still, if choice were available, there can be little doubt that most Chinese would want to enjoy the amenities, the stimulation, and the protection from nature that the "world" offers.

The United States was founded at a time when a static cosmos, with roots in classical antiquity and the Middle Ages, was being replaced by a confident scientific view of nature and a conception of history that stressed linear (progressive) change. The scientific view of nature itself could seem static in its perfection: outstandingly, Newton's system left that impression on many minds. Nevertheless, universal history rather than timeless laws of nature emerged as the dominant paradigm of thought in the eighteenth and nineteenth centuries, with science, especially in its applications, contributing to the sense of motion and progress.

America is the *locus classicus* of historical-geographic "master stories" or myths. Among the most powerful is the idea that civilization has marched westward, following the course of the sun, culminating in America. America as a whole is to be a City upon a Hill, a beacon of light (secular-moral, religious, and technological) to which people from other parts of the world are naturally drawn. Another powerful myth features the frontier. Opportunity lies "out there." This "out there" is both spatial and temporal. Four such frontiers can be identified: "land," "urban-manufacturing," "metropolitan," and "rurban-cybernetic" (Daniel Elazar). The earliest and most important of these, as concept and mythos, is the land or "agricultural" frontier. Open space and good soil beyond the horizon lure people westward. The urban-manufacturing frontier had its beginnings in the Northeast and then moved to the Midwest, where it remained for many decades. It boasts innovative procedures in extracting and transforming nature—nature not, however, as wilderness and land, but as steam and electricity, coal and iron. Its archetype is a technically minded tinker and inventor, someone like Thomas Edison, rather than a hardy farmer or rancher. The metropolitan frontier is a phenomenon of automated mobility—in particular, the car. It too brings people to the edge of nature, but only if they are scientifically trained and can probe the mysteries of the physical-biological universe. The rurban-cybernetic frontier is the latest to have emerged. Like the others, it has had its start in the Northeast, but has since established new growth centers in Illinois, California, and the Southwest. Nature, in this frontier, is remote indeed from the tangible things that one encounters in ordinary life. It has become an abstraction of chemical and physical properties, intellectually manipulated to create computers and technologies that have vastly improved the human ability to process and transmit information.[3]

Myths and reality are inextricably intertwined. The reality of America is created and maintained by overarching myths. Those called "historical-geographic"—in conjunction with the vocation of democracy—have persuaded many Americans to believe that no one need feel locked into place (a locality or a particular type of occupation), that there is always space out there where opportunity beckons, that there exists always a greater world into which one can move for fulfillment. This remains the dominant American creed: every major social change in recent history is intended to liberate a group from bondage to a fixed condition—to place.

Yet, in the past thirty years, a strong counterideology has emerged, one that seeks to restore place as the locus of human fulfillment. Many reasons account for this unexpected turn of events. I shall mention only two at this point. One is the development of a highly critical historical consciousness among leaders of thought: American history, they say, is not at all one of progress and enlightenment, as encapsulated in the four frontiers; rather it is one of greed, oppression, and gore committed against native inhabitants, imported slaves, poor immigrants, and nature itself. Restitution requires that nature regain some of its pristine luxuriance and diversity, that native inhabitants and ethnic immigrants rebuild their cultural heritage, taking more pride in it than in being, to use the language of Old Historians, the New Adam in a New World. The second reason for disaffection points again to the four frontiers. This time, however, the problem lies in their status not as powerful stories and myths but as reality. If only they were just myths! Myths can be quickly deconstructed, whereas reality takes longer. And what is the reality? It is that the frontier—the "cutting edge" where immigrants can establish themselves and proudly feel that they are contributing to the essential well-being of the larger society has long ceased to be "land," or even "steam and electricity" (manufacturing), but industries (biochemical, electronic, computer) based on esoteric science and knowledge, access to which requires years of schooling.

To reach a geographic frontier, one needs only a strong pair of legs; to reach an intellectual frontier, one needs a trained mind. Training the mind is not only arduous and expensive, with many risks of failure, it also inevitably takes one away from one's own kin group and homeplace, customs and beliefs, many of which originated in a pretechnological world of constraint. With the frontier now so remote, with furthermore the belief handed down from radical critics that science may not even be worth pursuing, being a sort of blight that decimates both natural and cultural diversity, it is understandable that migrants from poor countries, as well as Old Americans who harbor a deep sense of historical wrong and continue to suffer from ostracism, should find consolation in the hearth—in what they already have, enhanced on the one hand by heirlooms excavated from their own past and on the other hand by whatever material advantages a rich, high-technology society is able to offer.

Wanting to organize (say) a traditional harvest dance that shows a reverential, propitiary attitude toward nature and to do so with the help of research among historical documents, the telephone, and perhaps even the fax machine is paradoxical. Yet it is what ethnic groups in America, in their desire to retain a unique sense of self, do. And it is what many peoples in the rest of the world do, at different scales, including the scale of nation-state. Thus China not only wants to be both its historical self and modern like Sweden or the United States, it willingly uses all the modern tools of science—from historical linguistics to advanced methods of chemical dating—to re-create an authentic way of being "China and Chinese." What will happen when this paradox is fully and explicitly recognized?

Traditionalism, a return to some sentimentalized, unspecified past, is undesirable; in our global village, it is in any case impossible. Modernism is also undesirable in its "thinness," its often single (simpleminded) vision, its headlong rush to the new. That leaves us with high modernism, which sees merit in both "hearth" and "cosmos," Mole's cozy burrow with its reassuring mementos of the past and the open spaces with their promise of a different and more challenging future. However, in high modernism the two scales are not held in equal esteem: "cosmos" is favored. In this greater willingness to rank values and to defend the ranking with evidence and arguments normal to scholarly disputation, high modernism can be distinguished from certain extreme positions in postmodernism. The two modernisms have, of course, much in common: importantly, both show a playful and expansive spirit that is opposed to any kind of dogmatic creed, including that blind trust in reason in all areas of life that the West has inherited from the Enlightenment. But whereas such a playful and expansive spirit has led some postmodernists to radical relativism, the position that one form of life or culture is as good as another, the only question left being (intellectually) "Which is more interesting?" and (practically) "What must I do to advance my favorite agenda?" such is not the intellectual-political position of high modernists.[4] They are less disillusioned and more influenced by modernism's optimism and program: hesitations and doubts notwithstanding, they retain a sense of direction. That direction—from hearth to cosmos and thence to the paradoxical

concept of "cosmopolitan hearth"—gives high modernism its te-
los and its seriousness.[5]

Autobiographical Sketch

The story I wish to tell in this book is told from a cosmopolite's
viewpoint, not only in the sense that it attempts a comparative
study of cultures and civilizations, but also in the sense that I
value the cosmopolite's viewpoint and the cosmopolite's way of
life. My hope is that more and more people will be able to share in
both. To admit a *personal* preference in a work with scholarly aspirations is itself a high modernist (and postmodernist) posture,
as is also the laying bare of the probable sources of one's preference in one's biography, even when one knows that in taking this
step one may sound, not cautionary, but defensive and egotistical.

Born in China, I left it with my family at age ten for Australia.
From Australia, when I was about fifteen years old, we went to
England. After obtaining a degree from an English university in
1951, I came to the United States for further study. And here I still
am, in the United States, some forty-five years later. My childhood in China corresponded to the period of war with Japan. We
were constantly on the move, escaping from the invading army.
We ended up in the wartime capital of Chongqing. The economy
had broken down. We barely had enough to eat even though father held a good civil service job. The elementary school I at-
tended was a single room attached to an electricity-generating
station. But what a cosmopolitan education we had! Elevating
stories from the Chinese, European, and American pasts: stories
about Isaac Newton, Louis Pasteur, Benjamin Franklin, and other
scientists that were meant to stimulate our intellectual ambition,
and moral tales, including, naturally, ones of filial piety, but also,

astonishingly, Oscar Wilde's "The Happy Prince," that were meant to make us children into sensitive and compassionate adults. The one thing I dreaded above all lay on our daily trek to school when we had to go through a village. Periodically (but too often for my peace of mind), we had to stop to let a funeral procession pass. The corpse was wrapped in a bamboo sheet, on top of which was tied a rooster, which served as an advance warning system to the carriers and mourners, for it would crow if the corpse stirred. I both dreaded and hated the funeral procession, which I came to identify with traditional culture and folk life, drenched in superstition and fear, compared with which school was liberation—a sunny world where we learned about a man who flew a kite to bring down electricity.

In Australia, I was at an age when I began to rebel against the institution of family, including my own, because of what I vaguely felt was its suffocating worldliness. A middle-class professional family like mine was almost wholly secular in outlook: it was geared to success, and success meant an awareness of the realities of power. Well-educated Chinese of my parents' generation distanced themselves from the murky domain of spirits and demons, but they also distanced themselves from any idea of transcendence—from what might lie beyond the reach of rational Confucianism on the one hand and of Western social science on the other. In my Australian school, which had a Church of England foundation, I encountered for the first time a transsecular outlook that broke all the rules of common sense as they would be understood by a reasonable Chinese. To me as a child, even more astonishing than the miracles were the radical challenges to the primacy of hearth and kinship. "Who is my mother? Who are my brothers? . . . Whoever does the will of God is my brother, my sister, my mother." And who is my neighbor? Not someone next door to whom I extend assistance because I may need his help next week, but a total stranger by the wayside who cannot be expected to help me in return. And who is this God? He, too, I found both comforting and liberating—comforting on account of his name, "Heavenly Father," and liberating because he rises so far above partisanship that he "makes his sun shine on the good and bad alike, and sends rain on the honest and the dishonest."

In 1946, at age fifteen, I arrived with my family at the heart of the British empire, London, which, though still under food rationing and poorly fed by Sydney's standards, projected an air of cosmopolitan excitement and world-political import that the down-under city lacked. In 1946, the founding of the United Nations the previous year was still a transfiguring event to the starry-eyed young, myself included. The emphasis on what all human beings shared and might aspire to, despite superficial differences of appearance and custom, sounded fresh rather than clichéd after the abominations committed by a Nazi Germany that openly and proudly embraced a primitivistic cult of race and soil. At Oxford University, which I entered in 1948, students were aglow with big political and philosophical questions. How to reconstruct the war-torn world was a large enough question, but even larger was "the meaning of life," for existentialism, both atheistic and religious, was much in the air and frequently excited students to interminable debates. "Is world government possible or desirable?" and "Is life absurd?" (Camus) represented the two poles—political and metaphysical—that engaged our minds and passions. We understood at the time that other great issues would emerge to

challenge future generations of undergraduates, but we had na-
ively assumed that these would remain at a comparable breadth of
scope; that is, they would be universal or perennial rather than
local or time-bound, and argued from common axioms and principles of reasoning rather than from an angry partisan point of
view.

In 1951 I landed in New York and traveled by train to my destination, Berkeley, California. Looking out of the window as the
train sped across the Great Plains and the Rockies, I experienced
another kind of liberation, reinforcing the ones I felt earlier, but
this time inspired by the landscape itself. England, no longer the
imperial and cosmopolitan center of my earlier impressions, became for me the endearing hearth I had left behind, and here I
was in the great open spaces of the New World. At Berkeley, my
desire to explore the unfamiliar, especially if it promised broader
horizons, was satisfied by my chosen subfield within geography.
I could have written my thesis on Chinatown—a reasonable
enough topic for a Chinese geographer in the Bay Area. Instead, I
chose to do my research on a strange desert landform (the pedi-
ment) in Arizona. I wonder how I would see the world now if I
had begun my career with the study of a place that for all its commercial busyness was a depressed ghetto: very likely today's ethnic
passions—the demand for hearths that are also bases of political
power—would make better sense. Of course, it doesn't take research to see that minority groups needed and need more power.
How that power should be used is a more difficult question. Af-
firming a group's heritage is one use, and an important one, especially when that heritage—that past—is darkened by so much
poverty and suffering, and darkened further by condescending

commentary. Still, there cannot be serious challenge to the proposition that, for the most part, power should be used to free people from their involuntary social-locational confinement, so that anyone who so wishes can move into and benefit from the cultural and intellectual riches of the larger world.

Beyond the outer edges of home base, one always risks encountering hostile looks, taunting words, and even physical aggression. I have known racial prejudice in Australia as a child, and in England and the United States as an adult. But the occasions when it raised its ugly head were few and far between. How could that be? Both my lower-upper-middle-class status (as George Orwell might put it) and my unconscious Chinese-civilizational chauvinism protected me against overt slights and, indeed, my own sensitivity to them. My livelihood was never at stake, or even my material comfort and convenience, only my dignity, and that took more than a verbal or gestural derogation to breach. When a businessman walked over to my table and gave me the apple pie he did not care to eat, I was astonished, offended, but also subtly pleased to have acquired a conversational gambit for the next departmental social function. It would never have occurred to my American friends to apologize for the businessman, because it would never have occurred to them to identify with him. We were the cosmopolitans, smiling at the presumption of an ignorant local.

Chapters 2 and 3—"China" and "The United States"—represent my attempt to explore the theme of cosmos and hearth in two civilizations that, at a personal level, have defined my sense of being and that, at an impersonal level, serve to illustrate the distinction between "traditional" and "modern," between a society that strove for stability (heavenly peace) and one that took pride in openness, and with such openness, the likelihood of heterogeneity, recurrent contentiousness, and change. In these two chapters I write in the vein and with the sense of complexity of a seeker after knowledge. Objectivity remains my ideal, though in this work I know that it is constrained not only by my background and scholarly deficiencies, but also by my desire to restore a balance between the two poles of "cosmos" and "hearth." It is "cosmos"—society, civilization, world—that now needs intellectual restitution, for it has suffered in recent decades from unprecedented assault by influential critics, who, unlike those of even the recent past (for example, Lewis Mumford and René Dubos in the United States), could see no good at all in the larger-scale human achievements.

The last chapter, "A Cosmopolite's Viewpoint," builds on "China" and "The United States," but goes far beyond them to consider some of the more general, beneficent characteristics of the "cosmos." I will do so by means of a succession of comparisons—culture as custom with culture as technology, communal bond with societal networks of impersonal service, narrow reciprocity with circular reciprocity and linear giving, traditional hearth with "cosmopolitan hearth." Will the principal points of this chapter seem true but commonplace, or untrue and subversive? I suspect that opinion will be divided. Curiously, I can find a certain satisfaction with both poles of judgment. For the first tells me that there is, after all, broad agreement, while the second reassures me that there is need for this chapter and this book.

2

CHINA

The theme "cosmos and hearth" has many resonances in Chinese culture and history. It is captured, for a start, in the terms *t'ien* (heaven) and *ti* (earth), a polarized pair that is also a commonplace of other cultures, often anthropomorphized as Sky Father and Earth Mother. The two powers—heaven and earth—are not quite equal by historic times. Heaven has a slight edge, to the extent that it is seen as masculine, in contrast to earth, which is feminine. It may be that in an earlier time, before the emergence of writing and cities, greater emphasis was placed on the fertile earth—on chthonian deities that governed all living things rather than on a distant sky god whose role in human life was less clear. In China, by the time the words *t'ien* and *ti* came into use, there was little doubt that heaven mattered more: it was heaven that provided the mandate, not the earth. *Ti* (earth) represented something more localized. But the Chinese have another term for earth, *tu*, the meaning of which is even more localized. *Tu* means soil, a specific locality on earth. *T'ien* and *ti* are thus not just a dialectical pair but also components of a hierarchy—*t'ien*, *ti*, *tu*—which in human-social terms translates into emperor (Son of

Heaven), the magistrates and other members of the governing class, and the people.

The distinction carries other meanings as well. *T'ien* and its junior counterpart *ti* constitute the formal-imperial core of Chinese civilization and cosmos. When Westerners speak of "the splendors" of the Chinese empire, they have that core in mind—its astronomical-astrological worldview, its rites and ceremonies, its architecture, literature, and art. And no doubt the Chinese, too, think of these things when they feel a conscious pride in their culture. At the opposite pole of "the splendors" is *tu* or soil, which evokes locality, homestead, and hearth. This is the nurturing root of one's being. Attachment to it is built on the unexamined foundations of biological life, the intimacies of childhood experience, the warmth of familial communions, local customs and practices, the unique qualities of place. Taoism has conspicuously elevated home and hearth into an ideal of the simple life, worthy of cultivation by the scholar-official who, in obedience to principle and conscience, withdraws from the world.

Tu, however, has certain negative connotations as well, namely, those of "earthiness" and "dirt." It draws up images of country folk who work close to the soil and whose horizons are limited by customs that, to the literati, may seem bizarre and superstitious. These negative views apply not only to Chinese peasants but to non-Chinese peoples generally. And here the distinction is more bluntly put as one between "civilized" and "barbarian." To the Confucian literati, who not only enjoy but contribute to the products of their high culture, non-Chinese peoples live a cruder, more limited life: true, they have their own customs, which in the case of powerful nomads to the north and northwest may even have to be adapted and co-opted for reasons of state, but they are commonly deemed either colorful and quaint, or execrable. In this chapter, I shall depict elements of high culture, compare and contrast it with folk culture, and then compare and contrast it with the cultures of non-Chinese (non-Han) peoples.

Cosmos

The Chinese cosmos is a complex ordering of reality that has endured for more than two millennia. It has historically affected many areas of life, including administrative procedures, agricultural ceremonials and rites, architecture, literature, how people think and feel, how they relate to nature and society, and their whole sense of value and of appropriateness. Naturally, this cosmic edifice in all its grandeur and richness affects the elite most, but ordinary people too have come under its pervasive influence, though in a more fragmented, simplified, and dramatized form.

The principal lineaments of the Chinese cosmos may be summarized as follows. Space is organized by a grid of cardinal points and center, to which are attached a host of elements, including color and animals, the seasons, the substances (metal, wood, water, fire, earth), and human occupations. The spatial grid is also a vast cosmic timepiece, marking daily and seasonal changes. East is sunrise and spring; south, noon and summer; west, sunset and autumn; north, night and winter. Overarching the spatial grid and its elements are the two basic principles of the universe—yin and yang: yin the half cycle of shadow, dormancy, and death; yang the half cycle of light, life, and growth.[1]

This complex system of symbols and correspondences is a conceptual "edifice." But it is not just a richly articulated concept that one finds only in literary canons. It is also architecture—a tangible presence at various scales, from the monumental city to the palace and humbler residences. The capital city, with its walls oriented to the cardinal points, its palace and governmental complex at the center, is an imposing cosmic diagram. The emperor on his throne turns his back to the north and faces south—the sunlit world of human beings. In imperial audiences, civil officials enter the courtyard from the east, the direction that resonates with life (sunrise, spring, green, wood, blue-green dragon), whereas military officials enter from the west, the direction that carries connotations of dormancy or death (sunset, autumn, white, metal, white tiger). The north, which lies in the shadow or yin quarter of hibernating reptiles and the element water, is the appropriate locale for the profane activities of commerce.[2]

The Chinese cosmos has its origins in an agricultural way of life that depends for its sustenance and prosperity on soil fertility and climate. Rituals mark the changes of seasons, the shifts in the cycle of plant life from seedlings sprouting in spring, to summer growth and fall maturation and harvest. Even governmental activities may be geared to the alternations of yin and yang, the warm seasons of life (spring and summer), during which executions are banned, and the cool seasons of dormancy and death (autumn and winter), during which executions may take place. The solstices are critical points of transition: for several days before and after each solstice, governmental activities come to a halt to forestall the possibility of deleterious human interference.[3] Thus conceived and elaborated over the centuries, the Chinese cosmic edifice is a grand work of intricate harmony, imbued with a sense of rightness that is both aesthetic and moral.

Abstraction and Placelessness

The Chinese cosmos is magnificent and stately, the product of a society that believes in orderly (bureaucratic) organization and procedures. It has no nature divinities that go periodically berserk, like those in ancient Mesopotamia, nor Olympian gods and goddesses who behave much like willful human beings.[4] Yet it is also clearly premodern. The thought process behind it emphasizes correspondence and resonance (analogy and metaphor) rather than causality, as in modern thought. Nevertheless, what distinguishes it from other premodern ways of thinking is its predilection to organize space abstractly. Specificities of place are disregarded in favor of an impersonal grid. This is true not only of the cosmic worldview, but also of certain ambitious attempts at spatial organization for practical purposes within that worldview. One of the earliest (ca. 1000 B.C.) and surely the most ambitious was the Duke of Chou's aspiration to divide the country into mathematical squares with the royal capital at the center. Of course he could not carry out such a scheme, but he, like many of his successors, did feel a need for clarity and standardization. And at scales smaller than the country it could be translated into reality. Two well-known examples are the rectilinear patterning of streets in the cities and the "well-field" system of partitioning cultivated land, with each field the shape of a square, forty acres in size. These geometric undertakings are possible only in a political culture that believes, over a period of some three thousand years, that (as Ray Huang puts it) "the infrastructure of a nation and society can be artificially created."[5]

The abstract nature of a cosmic edifice is also indicated by its essential placelessness. The edifice is self-sufficient. It is its own reference system, the center of which is not necessarily any particular locality such as a grove rendered holy by the presence of a goddess, or a rock sanctified by an epiphany. It can be anywhere. It does not recognize the genius loci. Indeed, the construction of a geometric-cosmic city has frequently called for the destruction of the genius loci—for the removal of villages and wooded areas, the diversion of streams, and the flattening of hillocks.[6]

Historically, the capital city of China was located in three principal regions—the Wei Ho Valley, the Loyang plateau, and the Beijing plain. Only at the Loyang site was the capital built, repeatedly, on the ruins of an earlier one, as though the site itself had significance. In the two other areas, the precise location did not matter; indeed, the site of an earlier ruined capital might be avoided as inauspicious. Great cities were raised rapidly and were often destroyed rapidly by human enemies and by fire raging through buildings made of wood. To the Chinese, it was as though the material reality of the city carried little symbolic import. What counted was the form. This emphasis on form rather than on substance and locality is another sign of a shift away from the earth and earth deities toward heaven (astronomy-astrology) and the abstract.[7]

Rationalist Dispositions

I would like to continue with the idea that traditional Chinese culture exhibited, historically, certain rationalist tendencies. As I have already observed, these included a wish to organize space geometrically and a lack of attachment to specific sites. I now add to them a proclivity to favor commonsensical over magical interpretation of events. One can understand such proclivity as a mark of confidence, which the possession of power imparts. A confident society is one that commands power in regard to other societies and to nature. Imperial China has known that power. It deemed its neighbors inferior in culture and inferior even in military strength, though events often proved otherwise. Imperial China also confronted nature boldly. There was respect, but also disregard; for China, like other civilizations, had sought to control and transform nature in major ways. China's first emperor, Ch'in Shih Huang-ti, was egregiously superstitious because, reasonably enough, he could see that at least one part of nature—his own life span—lay beyond his ultimate control. External nature was, however, another matter. He considered himself superior to the minor deities of mountains and streams. He is said to have dispatched three thousand prisoners to deforest a mountain after he had been informed that the goddess there was responsible for the strong wind that impeded his river crossing.[8] True, he was enough a man of his time to believe in a goddess, but she certainly did not awe him. Generally speaking, since antiquity the Chinese governing elites (from the emperor down), by aligning themselves with the majesty and inexorable motion of the stars, had consistently shown a tendency to ride roughshod over the earth—including the spirits of the earth—when it suited their purpose to do so.

A rational bent marked Chinese society to the degree that it was Confucian. Confucius himself proclaimed agnosticism in otherworldly matters. "Devote yourself to human duties," he said. "Respect spiritual beings but keep your distance from them." When directly challenged on proper behavior toward spirits and life after death, he replied: "Until you are able to serve men, how can you serve spiritual beings? Until you know about life, how can you know about death?"[9] It was a duty of the Confucian magistrate, by example if not by proscription, to wean the common people from an excessive dependence on ghosts, spirits, and omens.

Ritual lay at the heart of Chinese society. But must not ritual be grounded on supernatural foundations? How could a particular gesture or practice have force and authority unless it was divinely sanctioned? Chinese thinkers, even in ancient times, did not appear to hold that rituals, whether conducted primarily to propitiate nature or to harmonize human relationships, were necessarily of divine provenance. Hsun-tzu (third century B.C.), for example, credited their establishment to kings of antiquity, who found them useful in the sociopolitical economy of curbing unruly human desires, contentiousness, and strife. Hsun-tzu also thought that ritual behavior satisfied deep emotional and aesthetic needs. He envisaged a loyal minister who had lost his lord or a filial son who had lost his parent. Such a person, even in the midst of enjoying himself in congenial company, might suddenly be overcome by sadness, which, unless it found expression in ritual gesture, could transmute into a sense of profound frustration and unfulfillment.[10] Ritual appealed to our aesthetic desires, too, according to Hsun-tzu. "Meats and grains, properly blended with the five flavors, please the mouth. Odors of pepper, orchid, and other sweet-smelling plants please the nose. The beauties of carving and inlay, embroidery and pattern please the eye. Bells and drums, strings and woodwinds please the ear. Spacious rooms and secluded halls, soft mats, cushions, etc., please the body. Therefore I say that rites are a means of satisfaction."[11]

It may be that in all societies the multitude of sensory-aesthetic delights that ritual and ceremony can offer are a major reason (largely unrecognized) for their popularity and endurance. What is noteworthy in China is that, so long ago, such very human satisfactions were explicitly recognized. Ritual as magical potency seemed far indeed from Hsun-tzu's thought. And if disenchantment was already under way in ancient China, we can expect it to have gone further in later times, especially during the great dynasties of power and cultural efflorescence, such as the T'ang (618–917). In the course of the T'ang dynasty, enlightened officials stressed again and again the human provenance of ritual. They were particularly anxious to prevent its pedantic and showy elaboration—an unfortunate consequence of human vanity but one that was palmed off as the need to abide by sacred tradition—by stressing its origin in human sentiment. Thus, in a memorial to the emperor T'ai-tsung, officials charged to investigate ritual opined bluntly: "It does not descend from Heaven, nor does it spring from Earth. [It is based] only on human feelings."[12] This being so, it must be flexible enough to accommodate changing feelings and attitudes. The emperor himself was impatient of obscurantist antecedents. When a counselor objected to the site the emperor had selected for the annual spring plowing ceremony because it was not sanctioned by ancient practice, T'ai-tsung responded: "Since rituals arise out of human feelings, how then can they remain permanent?" And here is an incident that vividly illustrates the emperor's disdain for omens and auspicious signs. When courtiers congratulated him for the appearance of albino magpies on the palace grounds, he became enraged, exclaiming: "A worthy man is indeed an auspicious omen. How can white magpies be beneficial to our affairs?" He forthwith ordered the nests torn down and the birds released to the wilds.[13]

Cosmic Space versus Sacral Places

Even in a well-ordered modern society, life remains uncertain at a personal level. Accidents can always happen, wiping out in a moment all the security and routine comforts that one takes for granted. T'ai-tsung's action, tearing down the nests of birds of good omen, is a bold act even by modern standards, for few of us even today are wholly unaffected by superstition. While this is true, it is also true that our society-and-space is overwhelmingly secular. What about traditional China? Its society-and-space was not secular as ours is, but it was not exactly sacred either. One way to gain an impression of its complex nature is to see it as consisting of two interpenetrating components—cosmic space and sacral places, the one maintained by the elite, the other by the people. Beijing, a symbol both in its totality and in its parts, was a splendid architectural example of cosmic space. To live there and respond to its symbols would be to participate not only in a human world but in the eternal cycles of nature. The experience might not be sacred, but it did have one characteristic of the sacred, namely, intimation of something beyond the mundane.

Cosmic space and its rituals were integral to officialdom, although not confined to it, for their influence permeated to people in humbler occupations. Nevertheless, ordinary people had their own experiences of sacredness quite different from those of the elite. The differences were in scale and in the degree of personalization. Beijing might be a cosmic diagram to the elite, but to ordinary people what mattered was not so much the whole as the parts—a particular temple, segment of wall, bridge, tower, tree or well. Sacrality manifested itself at specific points (places) within cosmic space. Again, in contrast to the impersonality of cosmic space, sacral places owed their numinous character to dramatic events and personages. Unlike the symbols and systems of correspondence that made cosmic space resonate, colorful stories enlivened sacral places. Take one such story, which grew around the huge bell in the Bell Tower located in the northern section of Beijing. Workmen assigned to cast the bell found mysteriously that they could not do so. Failure was punishable by death. To propitiate the spirits, a young maiden, daughter of the foreman, was thrown into the molten metal. Thereafter, casting presented no further difficulty, and the workmen were able to escape punishment. In time, the maiden herself was honored as a patron spirit by the people who lived near the tower.[14] This story and its variant versions, through repeated telling, had humanized a particular locality—and, indeed, made it seem superhuman—by making listeners believe that it literally incorporated a maiden at its core.

Sources of Pride

What were the sources of Chinese pride? Holy places might be local sources of pride: people who lived close to the Bell Tower, for example, had a story to tell, which gave them a certain cachet, but it would have to compete with other empowering stories. Every locality probably had something to boast about, but were there also broad cultural achievements, national traits, of which at least the educated Chinese were consciously or subconsciously proud? I believe there were. One was the numerical size of a people who shared, for all the minor differences, a common language, culture, and way of life. Another was the scope and grandeur of material culture: already in place by the fourth and third centuries B.C. were large walled cities, vast irrigation networks and canals, productive, intensively fertilized fields, and tree-lined roads that radiated from the capital city to the farthest corners of the empire. More deeply buried, as a source of pride, was military power. People in the capital and other great cities no doubt rejoiced as reports of military success came in from the frontiers. But none of the facts and accomplishments I have mentioned so far produced much public vaunting. For a number of reasons, the moral guardians of society—the scholar-officials and philosophers—could not give them wholehearted approval. Population size? Taking pride in it as such would have seemed childish, though, of course, at the family level there was indeed pride in numbers. Material culture? Yes, but great architectural works conflicted with the ideal of harmonious relationships with nature. As for military power, the Chinese state was exceptional among great states in belittling the naked assertion of will: its tradition lacked a warrior ethos.

So what aspects of culture were the Chinese unreservedly proud of? I believe there were two: the harmonious cosmos with its attendant rituals and Confucian humanism. These two aspects of culture had different origins but were in time so closely interwoven that they could be regarded as one, with the difference being largely whether attention was directed primarily to nature (adapting to the rhythms of heaven) or to human relationships (Confucianism). I have already sketched the moral-aesthetic character of the cosmos. Let me turn now to Confucianism, which too is a moral-aesthetic achievement. Its key concepts are captured by the terms *jen*, *li*, and *te*. *Jen* is the natural impulse toward the good—the good that is manifest in human relationships. *Jen*, though natural to human beings, is worth little undeveloped: it has to be (as Confucius put it) "cut, filed, carved, polished." In the Confucian view, a true human being and worthy member of society is one who has undergone a long and demanding course of education. Now education, though it calls for writing skills and learning the classics, is fundamentally the acquisition of *li*. What is *li*? Its root meaning is something like "holy ritual" or "sacred ceremony." Confucius's originality lies in extending this specialized meaning and high function to cover just about every aspect of human behavior—and behavior, whether it is a smile, a nod, or a word, inevitably engages and affects another person. Human behavior is human relationships, and human relationships can be endlessly refined so that *jen*, that natural impulse to good, can find full and appropriate expression wherever people meet. Every right gesture is *li* manifest and partakes of the holy. It has power or *te*. *Te* is virtue and it is also power, but not the power of manly aggression or virility, as in the West; rather it is the power that inheres in righteousness and holiness. Thus from the Confucian point of view, which has come to be the Chinese point of view in its most exalted form, human relationships in a civilized society rest not on any sort of physical or aggressive force but on the force (*te*) that flows naturally from right behavior, right action, or right inaction—a moral-aesthetic force that derives from the practice of *li*.[15]

Cosmic Menagerie

Cosmic harmony and Confucian humanism are the most refined and, in some ways, also the most distinctive achievements of Chinese culture. To moralists, they alone have an unambiguous claim to pride. But China was also a worldly empire, its emperors were potentates, its courtiers and officials connoisseurs of prestige even as they were connoisseurs of art. And so, to render my picture of China more complete, certain worldly components—cosmic menagerie (as distinct from cosmic harmony) and the secular world of strangers in the marketplace (as distinct from the ritualized behavior of Confucian humanism)—need to be added. And in making these additions, I bring out another meaning of cosmos. It is not only a harmonious, formal structure; it is also heterogeneity and plenitude. The two aspects of cosmos do not necessarily conflict, for the plenitude of elements may be agreeably arranged; in actuality they often do conflict, with the heterogeneous elements—strangers from all parts of the world—threatening the integrity of the whole. Partisans of the harmonious whole (officialdom and Confucian literati) thus view heterogeneity and plenitude with ambivalence: the wealth they indicate is not altogether compensated by the potential for disorder.

Cosmic menagerie poses little threat to the potentate. Indeed, it is one of the most effective symbols of his power. In all parts of the world, the potentate demonstrates the extent of his dominion by bringing into his capital, under his gaze, plants and animals from the "four corners of the earth." Thus Queen Hatshepsut of Egypt sent collecting expeditions as far away as Somalia that brought back with them exotic plants, including the tree that produced frankincense, and a vast array of animals for her palace zoo, among them monkeys, greyhounds, leopards (or cheetahs), hundreds of very tall cattle, many species of birds, and a giraffe. King Solomon kept great herds of domesticated animals such as beef cattle, sheep, and horses, but also traded exotic zoo animals with King Hiram of Tyre (I Kings 10).[16] As for China, the founder of the Ch'in dynasty (221–207 B.C.) walled off a vast hunting preserve near his capital in which he domiciled the rare beasts and birds that came as tribute from vassal states:

> Unicorns from Chiu Chen,
> Horses from Ferghana.
> Rhinoceros from Huang Chih,
> Birds from T'iao Chih.[17]

The potentate's cosmic menagerie highlights two aspects of power. One is the promotion of placelessness: plants and animals are uprooted from their native habitats and transported, perhaps over hundreds and even thousands of miles, to an alien environment where they are expected to mix harmoniously. The second aspect is this: whereas the potentate-gardener has near absolute control over the exotic plants, arranging them however he wishes, he has no such control over exotic animals, which can rarely be made to lie down side by side in peace. Now, if animals cannot be controlled unless they are put in cages, what about human beings? This question has special application to Ch'in Shih Huang-ti (founder of the Ch'in dynasty), for he not only uprooted plants and animals, but also the human rivals he had vanquished: he forced them and their families to destroy their houses, leave their fiefdoms, and move to the capital, where they had no base of support and where they would come under the Ch'in emperor's surveillance. The emperor's cosmic menagerie thus included human vassals as well as plants and animals. For him, no doubt the greatest source of unrest lay in his human vassals.[18]

World of Strangers

The cosmic menagerie may well be described as a world of strangers, since all its plants and animals are strangers to one another, not part of any natural biotic community. The strangers (the exotics) in a menagerie are, of course, there by force. In contrast, the strangers in a city are there by choice. A city with many strangers, coming from different parts of the world, is a cosmopolitan city. Cosmos as formal order and cosmos as heterogeneity and plenitude (cosmopolitanism) are in conflict. Formal order (the hierarchical establishment) sees itself threatened by heterogeneity, and heterogeneity sees itself threatened by all the legal means of coercion at the disposal of established order.

Consider Ch'ang-an, capital of the T'ang dynasty. As a traditional cosmic city, Ch'ang-an, for all its size and splendor, was designed for familiars—kith and kin writ large with the ruler (a father figure) at their head. Residents fell under the broad categories of court, officialdom, artisans and traders who catered to their needs, and farmers. Each group had its particular place in the order of things. Farmers and farming were integral to the cosmic city. Those who entered one of the gates along the city wall were more likely to encounter vegetable gardens and cultivated fields than streets and shops.[19] Agricultural life was ceremonially incorporated into court rituals: both had a cyclical character that reflected the cycles of nature. But the T'ang dynasty was a time of great economic vitality. Regional and international trade flourished as never before. Many cities attracted overseas visitors. Canton, for instance, grew to be a city of two hundred thousand, with ships belonging to Hindus, Arabs, Persians, and Malays sailing into the estuary, loaded with aromatic drugs, and other rare and precious goods.[20] Ch'ang-an itself, at its greatest, had a million people. Foreigners included not only the Arabs, Persians, and Hindus who were commonly found in the South, but also strangers from the North and West—Turks, Uighurs, Tocharians, Sogdians, Syrians, Tartars, and Tibetans. At its peak, no fewer than two thousand foreign trading firms operated within the city walls. Of course, not all foreigners came for trade: many were drawn to the city's culture—to the National Academy, for instance, which in the latter part of the seventh century boasted eight thousand students, of whom half were Chinese, and the other half consisted of Koreans, Japanese, Tibetans, and students from Central Asia.[21]

Diversity and Tolerance

Here, in medieval Ch'ang-an, were the seedbeds of a cosmopolitan world of tumultuous diversity. Cosmopolitanism implies tolerance, and there was enough tolerance for the multinational population to conduct business with and live close to one another in peace. Merchants needed to overlook ethnic-cultural differences in order to engage in activities of mutual benefit. Moreover, when the sun shone and livelihood seemed secure, the city's inhabitants surely went beyond mere tolerance to actively enjoying the vitality and color of life in a booming marketplace. What would we find if we could go there? We would find, according to one modern scholar, "a busy, raucous, and multilingual cluster of bazaars and warehouses, whose visitors were also entertained by prestidigitators and illusionists of every nationality, not to mention story-tellers, actors and acrobats."[22]

The T'ang dynasty marked a peak of Chinese culture. Although Islamic Baghdad and Orthodox Byzantium were notable cosmopolitan cities in the period 600 to 900, no Western city could remotely match Ch'ang-an in size and splendor. T'ang China's pre-eminence was cultural as much as it was military and political: witness the number of foreign students at the National Academy and the flourishing schools of art and literature. Yet it was in this time of ascendancy, rather than in times of barbarian pressure and doubt, that China was most open to alien influence. Turkish influence in the military sphere was especially strong, owing no doubt to the Turkic military origins of the dynasty's founder. Great landowning Chinese families along the frontier considered it a duty to have one son brought up to speak Turkish so that he could command Turkish troops in imperial service. The influence went beyond the military. Poetry, for example, might be chanted in a rhythm of Turkish derivation. Other than Turks, all sorts of people from Central Asia and points west settled in Chinese cities, bringing with them religions that the Chinese adopted, including Buddhism, Islam, Nestorian Christianity, Manichaeism, and Zoroastrianism.[23]

Of foreign religions, Buddhism had by far the greatest influence. Spreading rapidly through the country in the first centuries of the Christian era, it was by the fifth century (Northern Wei dynasty) almost a state religion. There existed then 47 grand state monasteries, 839 temples and monasteries of princes and eminent families, and 30,000 temples of the people.[24] Unlike Confucianism and Taoism, Buddhism penetrated all layers of society, so that during a Buddhist festival there was more than the usual sense of "heterogeneity and plenitude." People both high and low mixed in happy celebration, as the following account, written by a contemporary observer, shows. The occasion was Buddha's birthday, the place the Northern Wei capital of Lo-yang. A thousand images of Buddha were carried to the palace for the emperor to review:

Golden flowers sparkled in the sunlight, ornamented parasols floated about like clouds, the banners and pennants formed a forest, fumes from the incense resembled the mist, music and chants resounded and shook heaven and earth. Joy and play were in full swing, with the dense crowd milling around everywhere: eminent monks and virtuous elders formed groups carrying their walking sticks while faithful laymen assembled, holding flowers in their hands. Carriages blocked all thoroughfares, causing bewildering confusion everywhere.[25]

Order and Control

Magnificent order is one central idea of cosmos. A person in tune with it—courtier, scholar, or farmer—is a cosmopolite. Such order, however, is a product of will and of a logical, simplifying (abstracting) intelligence that is at odds with the biological needs of the body and the teeming, multifarious, passionate, and chaotic thrusts of life. Court ceremonial, for instance, is a type of cosmic order that can be maintained in splendor only through discipline, with no compromise with human weaknesses.[26] On a larger scale is the ideal of a harmonious city, whose material embodiment was a monumental walled compound. Walls defined space. Beyond the city walls lay the natural and human forces of anarchy, within them the heavenly and human forces of order. However, within the enceinted city were other walls—those of the quarters (*li* or *fang*) and those of individual residences. Some modern historians believe that the government used nested partitions to control residents as well as external enemies. Markets, where strangers congregated in large numbers, posed a special threat, and were for this reason tightly regulated. Their activities were confined to certain quarters and within stated hours. In the early part of the seventh century, quarter gates throughout the city of Ch'ang-an were closed after dark, and until the year 636 they were opened at dawn to the shouts of a military patrol.[27] The T'ang poet Po Chu-I depicts the city as an eerily empty nightscape, in which the houses are arranged like pieces on "a great chess-board," and the rectilinear streets a huge field "planted with rows of cabbage." In the distance the poet sees the flickering lights from the torches of riders to court, which are "like a single row of stars lying to the west of the five gates."[28]

Attempts at rigid control became more and more difficult in the face of commercial dynamism. A relaxation of rules occurred in the second half of the eighth century. The gates of the commercial quarters were permitted to stay open at night. Temporary markets emerged outside the city walls, next to the gates, and eventually merchants started to establish shops in the city but outside the quarters authorized for commerce.[29]

It is clear that the cosmic city of Ch'ang-an was yielding to the rising tide of cosmopolitanism. It could afford to do so, especially in regard to commerce, for the merchants were never a serious challenge to governmental prestige and authority. They did not constitute an independent estate and power. But religious adherents were another matter, and this was especially true of the numerous and best-organized group—the Buddhists. Chinese authorities tried to co-opt the Buddhist religious establishment, and to a remarkable degree they succeeded. Buddhism was Sinicized and integrated into the dominant Confucian tradition, and it was subject to the control of the secular elite: for example, the Ministry of Rites supervised the examination not only of Confucian scholars but also of Buddhist clerics. On the other hand, Buddhism did not simply spread within the preexistent social and institutional order. It had its own corporate communities, some of which acquired great wealth and claimed autonomy from governmental control and exemption from taxation. A religion that showed such signs of independence and that, moreover, could attract dedicated youths from good families, withdrawing them from filial obligations and secular service, posed a severe strain on both official and nonofficial tolerance, breaking it from time to time. Throughout the ninth century Buddhists suffered persecution, culminating in widespread violence in 845. Land was confiscated, and at the height of the violence, sanctuaries were destroyed, canonical works publicly burned, and numberless priests and nuns murdered. Buddhism suffered the most, but other non-Chinese faiths were also subjected to persecution.[30]

Local and Non-Chinese Cultures

Chinese culture—or to use the more restrictive term, Han culture—is remarkably homogeneous over an area of continental size, and it has been that way for thousands of years. The Chinese elite, surveying the empire from the capital, may well see the homogeneity as evidence of the natural acceptance of a superior civilization by people everywhere, whether ethnically Han or not. Within that broad uniformity, the cultured Chinese are aware of difference. Not only that, they appreciate it: they value the unique personality of places. "What is your native place?" is invariably the opening gambit of a conversation with a stranger. Locality, where one's ancestors are buried, reveals a person's identity and it is the source of his own deepest sense of self. Everyone takes a quiet pride in his or her homeplace, however humble; and the sophisticated elite are no exception. Each locality is assumed to have its own qualities, to which a native is permitted to draw attention, in a subtle and modest way, when he is in cosmopolitan company. These qualities may include a topographical feature or product, a certain accent and use of words (dialect), or a poetic or painterly style. It hardly needs saying that the differences are minor and never transgress the tacitly agreed upon rules and customs of propriety within the larger Han culture.[31]

I have been speaking of the elite. As for the peasants, who make up the bulk of the population, their practices too show a remarkable degree of uniformity, as numerous visitors, including social scientists, have observed.[32] Uniformity is prominent in family organization, modeled after that of the elite, and in the rituals that support the family, outstandingly, those that nurture filial piety. To be moral is to follow *li*—the gestures and rituals propagated by the privileged class, and instilled in village communities by the magistrate, who serves as the parent figure. Of course, peasant practices do not exactly replicate those of the elite. Magical and supernatural elements play a more prominent role in village ceremonies and festivals. They are tolerated by local officials, who see a belief in the supernatural and the bizarre as the effect of a lack of Confucian education and enlightenment. Where different customs occur, usually in the less accessible parts of remoter provinces, they suggest incomplete assimilation—that is, the presence of populations, originally non-Han, that became Sinicized but not in all respects.

The history of China, like that of many other countries, may be viewed as one of population growth and internal migrations, filling up niches and transforming them. From time to time, the Han people who lived in the Huang Ho basin migrated southward en masse to escape from wars and rebellions, human enemies and natural disasters. The first of these movements occurred with the breakdown of the Han empire in the third century, and others followed at irregular intervals to as late as the Ming and Ch'ing dynasties. As the people moved out of the cultural hearth into the less developed South, they retained as much of their prestigious heritage as possible, to the extent of inventing lineage ties when, with the passage of time, these could no longer be ascertained.[33] Many of the smaller non-Han tribes in South China, surrounded and numerically overwhelmed by the immigrants, succumbed to the lures of a more advanced and esteemed way of life, and turned themselves into Han Chinese. Modern ethnographers who went to subtropical China to conduct field surveys in the hope of ascertaining its ethnic complexity were often frustrated, for almost all the tribes there vigorously denied their non-Han origins, claiming instead that they had migrated from a northern province, and a few, to bolster their claim to authentic Chineseness, pushed their descent all the way to the legendary Yellow Emperor.[34]

Military Prowess, Cultural Backwardness

Tribes in south China tended to be small in size or weakly organized. To the southwest of the Han ecumene, however, were peoples, numerically significant, who matched China in military power. They could not be swamped. Yet they could be impressed by Han culture and wished to adopt, selectively, its ways. Consider the seventh and eighth centuries, a time when T'ang China, for all its cultural efflorescence, still had to contend with two rival powers—Tibet and Nan-chao. Tibet's great unifier, Song-tsen-gampo, was sufficiently admiring of Chinese culture to ask the T'ang emperor, T'ai-tsung (627–650), whether he could send his sons and younger brothers to study in Ch'ang-an. T'ai-tsung, for his part, considered it expedient to offer the Tibetan ruler an imperial princess as his bride. The Chinese bride, along with the Nepalese bride, played an important role in introducing Buddhism to Tibet. From China, Song-tsen-gampo also requested silkworm eggs, information on the manufacture of wine, paper, and silk, and on the making of millstones and grinding-mills. His grandson imported tea from China, and tea-drinking, as many as seventy cups a day per adult, became Tibet's addiction. Tibet, however, was at least as much influenced by India, which had the advantage of being closer to Tibet's population nodes.[35]

The T'ai kingdom of Nan-chao, centered on modern Yunnan province, was closer to China and had come under its political and cultural sway. But it did so willingly, even aggressively. Chinese culture was a plunder of war. In 829, when a Nan-chao army occupied Ch'eng-tu, "it seized tens of thousands of youths of both sexes, artisans and artists, scholars, books and products, all of which were transported south to its capital. Nan-chao's admiration for the northern Han culture did not cease one whit, with all its enmity for the north." Such captures were repeated. For instance, in 831 Nan-chao forces returned and took four thousand prisoners, and again in 836 they took some three thousand prisoners.[36] Note that Nan-chao kings considered talented artists and artisans valuable loot, indeed more valuable than mere things, for with captured talent the good things could be endlessly multiplied. And, of course, these Chinese captives, once they settled down, became powerful forces for the spread of Han culture.

Military success clearly did not entail cultural ascendancy. China, in its long history, had repeatedly encountered military equals and superiors. Tibet and Nan-chao fought China to a draw, while time and again steppe nomads conquered north

China, and under the Mongols, the whole country. Rather than impose nomadic customs on the vanquished, the victors adopted Chinese customs and institutions. Such experiences were a source of China's invincible conviction that, whatever military weaknesses it might have, its artistic-literary and institutional culture was indisputably superior.

Attitudes to Non-Chinese Peoples and Cultures

An attitude of superiority caused the Chinese to regard the non-Chinese as barbarians. Logically, this should lead to an idealization of cultural purity: China could dispense but would not accept. In fact, despite claims to superiority, the Chinese historically have shown themselves quite willing to accept all sorts of foreign cultural products and ways, from furniture and musical instruments to religion. Moreover, at a more deliberative level and indeed as a matter of policy, the Chinese ruling class (outstandingly during the T'ang dynasty) might adopt a foreign style of dress, learn a foreign language, and establish kinship ties through marriage, so as to better influence and control what were called "allied tribes."[37]

As the empire expanded into new territories, how were the non-Chinese who lived there treated in practice? The answer is, varyingly, from extreme harshness to condescending benevolence and grudging respect, depending on their political-military power. The steppe nomads had to be handled with diplomatic finesse; likewise, the Tibetans and the T'ai during the T'ang dynasty. But harshness, even to the degree of engaging in wars of extermination, was all too common in regard to the less populous and organized tribes scattered throughout subtropical and tropical China. During the Ming (1368–1644) and Ch'ing (1644–1911) dynasties, for example, Chinese armies waged campaigns against the Miao and the Yao, driving them off their lands and massacring them to make way for Chinese settlers.[38] Survivors retreated into the hills and mountains to eke out a living in a territory considered of little value to the Chinese. This inhuman tale is not unfamiliar in other parts of the world. More distinctive of China, and less harsh, were two methods of establishing control or suzerainty: the military-agricultural colony and the vassal state.

As early as the Ch'in dynasty in the third century B.C., the Chinese established military-agricultural colonies in the frontier regions. The practice worked well enough for it to be applied again and again throughout China's imperial history. Soldiers were dispatched to pacify a region; they then settled down as farmers who could defend the region against displaced and disgruntled natives. The colonies served as centers of Chinese authority and for the diffusion of Chinese culture. Non-Han people in adjoining territories might adopt Han practices, especially those agricultural techniques that they could see were superior, and in time they became indistinguishable from the colonizers. Assimilation sometimes proceeded to the point at which, as we have noted earlier, the natives could no longer recall their own origins. On the other hand, where the indigenous population was large, the Chinese colonizers, isolated from their kind, might turn native. Cultural transfer was by no means unidirectional.

The second method of extending imperial influence—the establishment of a vassal state or protectorate—was applied to frontier regions too remote or, for some other reason, too troublesome for central control. Since the Chou dynasty, China adopted a policy of benevolence toward the non-Han, captured in the unselfconsciously condescending phrase, "Cherish the feudal princes, win the distant peoples by kindness and restraint." The court invited foreign chieftains for ceremonial visits, where they were treated to an impressive exhibition of Confucian etiquette and lavished with gifts, which outweighed in value the tributes that the visitors brought. The court showed concern in other ways as well, for instance, by sending congratulatory messages to a vassal state when it enjoyed good fortune, and condolences when it suffered calamities.[39] Given the fact that the Chou dynasty itself was feudal, establishing feudal ties with alien peoples seemed natural. In later imperial dynasties, this feudal relationship was modified in numerous details, but not in essential character. During the T'ang dynasty, hundreds of chieftains in south and southwest China willingly submitted to Chinese suzerainty. They accepted titles and trappings of office from the emperor, and flocked to the capital for imperial audiences. They did so not necessarily out of fear or even expediency. The prestige and possibly even the showmanship of such occasions led them to participate in the rites of imperial theater.

In the course of the Ming dynasty, ways of dealing with non-Han tribes in south China were progressively institutionalized. A system of administration that had a fully articulated hierarchy of ranks and rules came into use and was known as the *t'u-ssu* system. *T'u* means local or indigenous, and *ssu* means chieftain. The local and earthbound were clearly subservient to the cosmic pretensions of empire. Chinese authorities showed little serious interest in what the tribes did in their own territories: if information was collected it was as exotica and curiosities, or as observations of nature. Attention was directed to the tribes only when they came into conflict with Chinese farmers, usually over land. The *t'u-ssu* system made the non-Han peoples a part of the empire but not a part of the civilization. What did the Chinese official, ensconced in the refinements of his world, really think of the non-Han tribes? No doubt opinions differed, but a case can be made that they were usually patronizing if not contemptuous. Consider Wang Shou-jen (1472–1528), an official of great distinction who had administrative experience in Kwei-chou province, where many non-Han peoples lived. In his characterization of their chieftains (the *t'u-ssu*) and how to pacify them, he used a wildlife metaphor that showed his disdain:

> The proper way to treat the *t'u-ssu* is to adapt one's policy to fit their character. Divide their leadership in order to split up their unity. Establish civil service aides to supervise and control their power. These barbarians are like the wild deer. To institute direct civil administration by Han-Chinese magistrates would be like herding deer into the hall of a house and trying to tame them. In the end, they merely butt over your sacrificial altars, kick over your tables, and dash about in frantic fright.[40]

Modern Stirrings: Science and Democracy

By late imperial times, traditional Chinese culture has acquired, largely through its own internal debates and cogitations, certain attitudes and values that may be considered modern. Among the supporting evidences is a novel, *Destinies of the Flowers in the Mirror*, which, according to Mark Elvin, is a microcosm of the educated Chinese mind around the year 1830. The novel indicates that the Chinese have at last recognized that they are "Chinese," with customs that no doubt rise superior to those of other people, but which nevertheless are conventions of a particular time and place. A measure of cultural relativism is recognized and accepted. That men dress differently from women and have different social roles and power is considered ultimately arbitrary. A delight in technology appears throughout the novel, which represents a departure from the scholar-official's historical tendency to see technology as mere cleverness, a sort of trick, not on the same order of accomplishment as moral thinking and behavior (*li*). New, too, is the idea that the Chinese may offer technical assistance to less advanced peoples. Again, although the obsession with scholarship in the novel may be seen as traditional, the weight given to reason and to the soundness of an argument, as distinct from the writer or speaker's official standing (authority), is new and part of a critical trend that has its beginnings in the eighteenth century.[41]

Nevertheless, a radical reevaluation of Chinese culture and of China's place in the world came only after a succession of deeply humiliating defeats by European powers (beginning with the Opium War of 1839–42) and, later, Japan. A disposition in traditional high culture to favor common sense and the rational, and, in the eighteenth century, the emergence of a critical attitude toward the literary canons, prepared Chinese intellectuals to leap into the modern, even if this meant—for some—a decisive break with the past. Early in the twentieth century, a dean at Beijing University, the most prestigious in China, attacked Confucianism in the name of Western science and democracy. To his mind, Confucianism was responsible for the stultification of thought, which in turn led to the country's social and technological backwardness. In 1915, the New Learning movement sought to revise Chinese culture at its root by revising script and vocabulary. Scientific skepticism and method, their effectiveness so amply demonstrated in technical studies, were applied to literary studies. The result was not just the textual emendation of traditional scholarship or even the newer criticisms of the eighteenth century, but the raising of fundamental doubt concerning the provenance and authenticity of the classics and, with it, the factuality of early Chinese history.[42]

"Science and democracy" was the rallying cry of the student movement of May 4, 1919, in protest against the injustices of the Versailles peace treaty. Almost exactly seventy years later, under a different government and in a totally altered world, the student protesters of Tiananmen Square again used "science and democracy" as their rallying cry—a cry that sounded oddly abstract and was strikingly at variance with the ethnic and nationalist slogans of the 1980s in other parts of the world, which looked backward to cultural heritage and roots rather than forward to science and democracy. Chinese students at Tiananmen were protesting against a system—communism—that itself was of Western provenance and that in fact played a role in the original New Learning movement. And, of course, communism claimed to be scientific, based on the hard facts and the inexorable logic of dialectical materialism. However, to student protesters in 1989 and to increasing numbers of Chinese from the late 1970s onward, communism was not a science but a superstition clothed in pseudoscientific language, and it produced not a social heaven—a utopia guided by reason—but a rigidly authoritarian and increasingly inefficient state.

Village and Ethnic Cultures in the 1930s

Modernism attacks backwardness. There is the backwardness of high culture, symbolized by the rigidities of Confucianism. And there is the backwardness of village and ethnic culture. Considered as a way of thought, Confucianism, with its rationalist bent, stands less in the way of modernism than do the rooted habits and beliefs of villagers, whether Han Chinese or not. To put it somewhat differently, sacred space, with its cool abstractions, can more readily be discarded or transformed into modern space and organization than can sacral localities, with their grounding in the supernatural—in its dramatic narratives and enactments. In trying to understand what China has to overcome as it struggles to modernize and, moreover, in trying to understand the potential for violent conflict among ethnic groups, still anchored in their respective customs and beliefs, we need to examine specific cases.

Consider the three peoples of the Kansu-Tibetan borderland, which the anthropologist Robert B. Ekvall studied in the 1930s. They offer us a striking example of similarity and difference, cooperative living and seemingly irreconcilable conflict. The borderland, where the Tibetan plateau slopes down north- and eastward to fertile, loess-covered valleys, is located at the geographical center of the Chinese state. There, Han Chinese, Muslim Chinese, and Tibetans complexly interlace and mix, without losing their separate identities. What they have in common is easily stated. They all come under Chinese sovereignty, a fact that influences their political behavior and administrative structure. For all three, sedentary agriculture provides the basis of livelihood. The crops (principally wheat, millet, and barley) are raised for local consumption, and the rhythms of work, dictated by the seasons, are much the same. Tibetan villagers have more livestock, but even Han and Muslim villages maintain a few sheep, which are raised for lambskins. Although racial differences can be detected by a trained observer, they are not sufficient to be a source of daily awareness among the local people: the "us versus them" syndrome is based on cultural rather than on biological differences. The Tibetans and the Han Chinese look much alike; as for the Muslims, they have intermarried with the Han for so long that their Semitic features are much diluted, although still subtly discernible in the shape of the nose and the reddish tint to the hair.[43]

The Tibetans moved from the Lhasa region northward into the valleys of the Kansu-Tibetan borderland in the fourteenth century. The Han Chinese have been farmers in the lower valleys of the same borderland for millennia, but they migrated up—or were moved up as military-agricultural colonies—to the higher valleys, where they came into contact with the Tibetans, perhaps also in the fourteenth century, that is, early in the Ming dynasty. On the whole, the two peoples have lived together peacefully. Their respective cultures show differences and similarities. Religion dominates Tibetan life, but sits lightly on the Han. Religion, however, is not a source of friction. Buddhism, which both groups embrace, is not an aggressive and intolerant faith. Moreover, the religions of both the Tibetans and the Han are syncretic. Tibetan Buddhism (or Lamaism) is incongruously mixed with the older animistic religion of fierce gods and demons whose shrines dot the landscape. Tibetan villagers are not bothered by gross inconsistency between doctrine and practice, between (say) the prohibition against killing animals for meat and indulging in the delights of the chase and eating meat. As for the Han villagers, their religion is the traditional mix of Confucianism, Buddhism, and Taoism that can be found throughout China. A tolerant attitude to religion makes it easy for the Han Chinese to take on more Buddhist elements under the influence of their Tibetan neighbors and, again under their influence, to let religious concerns rule a larger portion of their lives.

Nevertheless, the general direction of cultural change in the higher valleys of the borderland is from Tibetan to Han. With the passage of time, Tibetan villages and villagers assume more of a Han Chinese character. Chinese political hegemony no doubt plays a role, but other factors are at work as well. Cultural prestige, for instance, probably accounts for the Tibetan adoption of the Han-style trousers and chopsticks. Practicality is another factor: the Chinese *kang*—the heated masonry platform or bed—enjoys a clear advantage over other means of keeping warm economically at high elevations.[44] Finally, Han but not Tibetan population is increasing rapidly. In some isolated villages, beyond the easy reach of Chinese immigrants, Tibetans are not even re-placing themselves. The shift in population and culture may be expected to cause ill-feeling. But this has not happened. Tibetan villagers do not seem to feel that they have been rudely displaced or that they have had to yield to Chinese customs under pressure. It may also be that they are not aware of any great cultural loss, because in the one area of fundamental importance to them—religion—they have changed little. A Tibetan community, in recognition of Han cultural superiority, may become so thor-oughly Sinicized as to be indistinguishable from Han communi-ties, except for its emphasis on religion. What religion—or rather, what facet of it? The answer is not so much the teachings and practices that are recognizably Buddhist, which the Tibetans in any case share with the Han Chinese, but rather an older, more primitive and fervent religion that is unique to them—the worship of mountain gods.[45]

In contrast to the peaceful relationship between Tibetans and Han, the relationship between Muslims and Han in the lower valleys of the borderland is typically wary and even hostile, erupting from time to time into open conflict. And this despite the fact that in all matters except religion they have much more in common: they speak the same language, and differences in material culture such as clothes, house, farm, and farm work, are slight. Muslims, in short, are Chinese—Muslim Chinese. Yet the two groups prefer to live separately. Villages in the same valley are either predominantly Chinese or Muslim. In the larger towns, where separation is less marked, Muslims tend to be concentrated in certain trades such as innkeeping, cartering, muleteering, and soldiering. Mixing, where it does occur, can be close-grained. In a Muslim teashop, for instance, one may find both Muslim and Han customers: the former are there in part for dietary reasons, the latter because they appreciate its cleanliness.[46]

The two groups live close enough to irritate each other—bitterly so when Chinese New Year happens to coincide with Muslim Ramadan. Consider what can happen. On the one side are the turmoil and high spirits of the New Year: exploding firecrackers, clashing cymbals and gongs, outdoor theatricals clangorously performed, gaudily dressed effigies of idols carried around the streets, pigs grunting in the village square, people gorging themselves with food. On the other side is the decorousness of a religious festival, during which long-faced Muslims fast and pray for thirty days. Under the provocation of even a minor incident, tempers flare and fists fly, ending in violent conflict that can involve whole communities.[47]

Religion is a fundamental cause of irreconcilability. Most Chinese, as we have noted, embrace Confucianism interlarded with Taoist and Buddhist beliefs. Peasants, however, know little of the philosophical abstractions and high ideals of these faiths. What they derive from them and elaborate on their own are images and effigies of supernatural powers, specific propitiatory practices appropriate to them, which tend to proliferate with time, and a general faith in the efficacy of magic. Confucian ancestors, Buddhist Bodhisattvas, and Taoist adepts have all been turned into figures that work wonders (idols), deferred to and worshipped to the degree that they produce results. Peasant deities are local deities, tied to place. They cannot move unless their effigies are carried around. During a time of drought, the effigy of a god may be taken out of his temple niche and given a tour of the fields to see the extent of the damage. If still no rain falls—that is, if the god is obdurate and refuses to do what is required of him—"he is left for hours in the burning sun so that personal discomfort may add its urgings to the prayer of the people."[48]

Attitude to the dead is a key part of religious culture, and here again the differences can be irreconcilable. To an elderly Chinese, the sight of a sturdy coffin by his side is reassuring, for it bespeaks filial piety and material well-being. Muslims, by contrast, see the coffin as a heathenish misplacement of faith in the power of materiality to guarantee afterlife. Their dead are wrapped in cloths and placed on shelves that have been dug into the sides of a trench. To the Han Chinese, this is burying human beings like one would dogs: only savages do that. Chinese funerals are a theater of emotional outpouring, yet once the dead are interred they are quickly forgotten. Burial mounds themselves are not fenced off or treated with any special respect; sheep and cattle are allowed to graze on them. By contrast, Muslim funerals are sedate, and they take pains to make their burial grounds look like parks, sanctified places for meditation.[49]

Religion, where taken seriously, penetrates all areas of life, including food and food taboos. A source of intense irritation between Han and Muslim Chinese lies in their attitude to the pig. Pork is the favorite meat among Han Chinese. In a typical village, pigs are everywhere—in courtyards and public squares, on roads and alleyways. Foodshops and butchershops proudly display slabs of raw or cooked pig. Pigs—alive and squealing or dead and strung up—severely provoke the sensibilities of the Muslims. To them, pigs are an offense to the eye, an abomination that pollutes ground and air. On the other hand, Muslims eat beef, whereas Han villagers consider cattle, which pull their plows and do other heavy work, objects of respect; in any case, they are not to be slaughtered for meat.[50]

Most of the time, the three peoples of the borderland live in peace. Tibetan and Han villagers, in particular, seem to adapt to each other's ways well. The relationship between Muslim and Han Chinese is less easy, as we have indicated: the two peoples have withdrawn more and more into themselves—into separate, almost exclusive villages, and then into separate, almost exclusive districts. Yet hostility is by no means always at the surface. Especially in the larger towns, mixing and a degree of socializing willingly occur. Chinese villagers like to visit Muslim teashops, and Muslims for their part can appreciate the liveliness of certain Han Chinese festivals even though they may participate only as spectators. Generally, differences in custom and behavior add to the colorfulness and vitality of a region: people can derive pleasure in neighbors who are nonthreateningly peculiar; for, after all, one of humankind's favorite pastimes—gossip—depends on the existence of difference and opportunities to comment on it in a lively manner.

The Larger Political-Cultural Contexts

The Han, Muslim, and Tibetan villagers of the borderland live in their own small worlds, which are also parts of much larger cultural-political entities. One of them—the most important—is the Chinese state and its government. Han villagers know that a central government exists, which rules over them through its officials and through the power of taxation. The villagers are also aware of a much larger, more sophisticated cultural world beyond the borderland, to which they belong. In the early decades of the twentieth century, they made attempts to raise themselves to a higher, more prestigious level under the prompting of the local elites. The move was in the direction of enlightened Confucianism, which on the one hand plays down the worship of local deities (kitchen gods, etc.), magical beliefs, and extravagant funeral rites, and on the other hand builds up filial piety and the well-ordered family—the foundation for society at large—based on genuine respect and affection and on an awareness of the mutual obligations and duties between the generations.

As for the Muslim villagers, they know that they are united by a common religion and that they belong to a large Islamic world beyond the borders of China. Such awareness, however vague, gives them a sense of confidence and power. In the twentieth century, Muslim leaders have risen to be governors and generals of Chinese provinces under the distant supervision of the central government. As de facto rulers of a sizable region, they are courted by political powers outside of China, and so are drawn into the world's ambitions and turmoils. Chinese overlordship of the borderland alternates between neglect and the arrogant assertion of control—or so the control seemed to Muslims in such matters as taxation, attempts to arbitrate their internal feuds, and treatment in the courts.[51] Rebellion, once it occurs, explodes into indiscriminate slaughter from both sides. The virulence of the killing would be hard to understand if one considers simply the initial political causes. What fuels it is something more psychological—the long-repressed irritation of cultural incompatibility that suddenly turns into open hatred.

Tibetan villagers in the borderland, like the other two groups, are aware of a larger cultural realm to which they belong. However, they identify less with Greater Tibet—a vague concept at best—than with their nomadic brethren on the nearby plateau, whose wealth in livestock and freer way of life are sometimes envied. Sedentary Tibetans, when they have achieved a certain level of well-being, may well abandon their tie to soil and become nomadic herders.[52] In this desire for mobility, they differ markedly from the Han Chinese. As for the influence of Lhasa on this borderland, it exercises its political right to send district officers there, but Lhasa does not automatically command the local people's sentimental attachment or loyalty. Indeed, bad feelings emerge when a Tibetan official, aware of Lhasa's remoteness, abuses his powers and treats his charges more harshly than would a Chinese magistrate. It is not unknown for a Tibetan village, already much Sinicized, to place itself voluntarily under Chinese authority.

The relationship between Tibet and China, though peaceful in this region in the 1920s and 1930s, has been strained and turbulent historically and since the communist government took over. I shall return to Tibet after considering first, more generally, China's attitude toward national minorities in the late twentieth century.

National Minorities

Twentieth-century China, in its effort to modernize, sees as its primary task the lifting of the peasant masses out of poverty. This calls for land reform and other economic changes, but at a deeper level it calls for their education; and education means not only literacy but a shift in the peasant habit of mind—away from magic and sterile customs to rational thought and freedom. Besides Chinese peasants, there are the non-Han minorities, who make up some 9 percent of the total population, many of whom, too, are enmeshed in poverty. What policy to adopt toward them? The question is a difficult one if only because culturally and in social organization the minorities are extremely diverse: included are (or were, until recently) head hunters, hunter-gatherers, pastoral nomads, monastic communities, societies of slave owners and slaves, lords and serfs. They differ greatly in power. Some are too small and splintered to resist Chinese domination, others are numerous and strong enough to challenge it.

In the twentieth century, China's policy toward the minorities has swung back and forth between total assimilation and varying degrees of circumscribed autonomy. Autonomy is essentially cultural rather than economic and political. In the Soviet (and communist) understanding of human reality, the cultural is superstructure: what matter and therefore must remain in the hands of the central government are the hard economic and political facts. The People's Republic, during the 1950s, had come under the in-

fluence of this point of view. It set up various types of autonomous regions and encouraged cultural diversity. Culture, however, meant such customs as folk dance, song, and dress, and
other colorful products and trappings that might appeal to tourists, rather than something deeply embedded such as religious
worship, social structure, and rules of property ownership and
distribution, which were bound to conflict with the government's
political ideology and economic program for the entire country.[53]

Encouragement of ethnic-cultural displays and festivals might
have received its most direct impetus and inspiration from Soviet practice. On the other hand, their roots are much older.
Potentates in all times and places have sought to exhibit their
power—their claim to being universal rulers—by bringing exotic
plants, animals, and, above all, people to their capital. The imperial British have done it with panache in royal weddings and
jubilees. Soviet and Chinese rulers have attempted the same
sort of ingathering during national holidays, though perhaps with
less theatrical flair.

The Cultural Revolution (1966–76) departed radically from this
earlier phase of paternalistic tolerance. "Cultural Revolution" is a
misnomer because, far from being a new assertion of cultural primacy, it was a herculean effort to suppress, in the name of puritanical reason, culture in all its diversity and luxuriance. Culture
signified backwardness. Not only religious worship but health
practices among minority groups and even traditional Chinese
medicine were declared "unscientific, feudal, and backward."
Languages and customs, folk dances and songs that once received
official support were all judged backward and divisive, holding
China back as a modern nation. Those who continued to find so-

lace in magical practices, those who participated in initiation rites and love feasts, and those who simply continued to speak and write in their native language were all deemed "counterrevolutionaries" and punished accordingly.[54]

Puritanical fanaticism, with its utter inability to accept difference, soon passed: it could hardly have lasted much longer without bringing the entire country to ruin. In 1984, the People's Republic promulgated a law that again turned to a more sympathetic view of minority cultures, going indeed further than the decrees of the 1950s by allowing greater autonomy. Under the new law, people in autonomous regions could regulate their own customs and traditions, language and writing, marriage and administrative procedures—all within (of course) the polity of the Communist party and government. Good as this sounds to the non-Han when compared with the denunciation and persecution of the 1960s and 1970s, does it go far enough? Just how much autonomy can any central Chinese government tolerate? For that matter, what do the national minorities themselves really want? Do they see their own future as cultural curiosities, living museum tableaux, or as participants in a transregional (even global) economy and communications network that will inevitably affect how they think and what they do?

The difficulty of this question to China's non-Han peoples has its source in their unresolved ambivalence toward modernization and economic progress. On the one hand, they strongly desire to rise to a level of material well-being commensurate with what they can see in the more developed parts of the world; on the other hand, they suspect that economic development will sooner or later weaken their own cultural traditions. A further complication emerges from internal politics. Even if the common people do not mind letting go of certain cultural habits in exchange for the affluence promised by modernization, their leaders, who have risen to power on cultural particularism and on the sacredness of the kinship-ethnic bond, understandably show reluctance. Ironically, ethnic leaders, for all their apparent devotion to localism, themselves deserve the title of cosmopolite, for their particular brand of localism—its savvy political thrust—owes much to a powerful ideology, worldwide in scope, that favors "difference," that makes "diversity" or "heterogeneity" into yardsticks for moral excellence. A further twist to the problems is this. In south China, where ethnic diversity is greatest, a Han community may claim to be ethnic even though scientific study shows otherwise. It makes such a claim in the hope of getting the government to protect its members against the predations of a rival group. It may also do so to gain certain economic and educational favors from Beijing.[55]

The Case of Tibet

Of all the ethnic peoples in China, the Tibetans have been most successful in catching the world's attention and winning the world's sympathy in their aspiration toward greater autonomy, if not outright independence. What, historically, was the relationship between Tibet and China? Why does the outside world, particularly the English-speaking world (both governments and peoples), show such persistent interest in Tibet? Why does China show such truculence and why does it seem almost bewildered and self-righteously indignant when its policies on Tibet are roundly condemned by the Western press? The first two questions

I will leave largely undeveloped: I need them only as background for the one question that I will attempt to address, namely, China's truculence and bewilderment. The source of this truculence and bewilderment lies, I believe, in the centuries-old conflict between cosmos and locality, harmonious order and teeming plenitude, a way of life that is essentially secular (Han) and a way of life that is not only religious but magical.

First, a sketch of the historical context. Tibet's earliest confrontations with China were as a military power, before Buddhism had penetrated and transformed its culture and society. Since that transformation, Tibet's relationship with China oscillated with China's military-political fortune. That fortune rose to a peak in the eighteenth century, when Ch'ing (Manchu) China firmly asserted its sovereign rights over Tibet. It fell to a trough in the second half of the nineteenth century, when China itself came under European hegemonic influence. Tibet, loosened from a weakened China, became a pawn to two European powers—Britain and Russia. Britain sought to put "fences" around the high plateau so that neither Russia nor China could include Tibet's strategic position and untapped mineral resources in its political sphere and thus pose a threat to British India. Britain would have liked to see Tibet turned into a sort of ethnic treasure house, with the British serving as curators.

This did not happen, but something like it did. In the nineteenth and early part of the twentieth century, Tibet was made into a myth—the Romantic Other for a Europe that had become highly industrialized, polluted, and disenchanted. Tibet was Shangri-la, with time frozen in an unspecified past, a land of monasteries, topped by one of the world's most widely recognized buildings (the Potala) and populated by devout monks, benign hierarchs, freedom-loving nomads and happy peasants, all suffused in a glow of Buddhist mysticism.[56] At the end of the twentieth century, this myth is as potent as ever, thanks in part to the arrogant secularism and political maladroitness of the governing Chinese, and in part to the winsome personality of Tibet's exiled Dalai Lama, who, in his travels throughout the Western world, has managed to portray his country as much like himself—deeply religious, yet untouched by fanaticism, part of a monastic hierarchy, yet fundamentally democratic.

People can be creatures of their own myth, or of a rosy image created for them by others. Thus, under America's own mythic rubric "All men are created equal," Americans did become in time more equal. And it may be that Tibet, in its need to set itself up as Virtue contraposed to China's Evil, has indeed become more virtuous in its social practices and enlightened in religion. If so, we have an example of good coming out of misfortune. But what was Tibet really like in the first half of the twentieth century? Some of the finer qualities attributed to it by myth were surely there, but other qualities or characteristics less fine, more ambiguous, and even reprehensible also existed.

Although material backwardness as such is nothing to be ashamed of, Tibet, as the country that had built the monumental Potala, was puzzlingly backward in material technology—other than that used in prayer wheels—right through the first half of the twentieth century. Traffic in people and goods was by riding on pack animals over rough, narrow tracks. Roads adequate to wheeled traffic hardly existed until the Chinese communist government built them. But then there were no wheeled vehicles of any kind! Heinrich Harrer, who spent seven years in Tibet (1943–50) as tutor to the Dalai Lama and who was most sympathetic to nearly everything Tibetan, nevertheless could not overcome his indignation when he saw how men sweated and panted as they dragged heavy tree trunks by means of ropes tied to their waists. Surely, Harrer said, there must be "some better means of transporting these heavy burdens than by manhandling them. The Chinese invented and used the wheel thousands of years ago. But the Tibetans would have none of it, though its use would . . . raise the whole standard of living throughout the country."[57]

The tree trunks were to be put one on top of the other to make a towering flagstaff for New Year celebrations in Lhasa. Carriers worked in successive teams. One team dragged the trunks between its village and the next one miles away, where another team took over, and so on to the other settlements and teams all the way to Lhasa. What I am describing here was forced labor. It constituted a kind of taxation and reminds us that Tibet was a feudal society until recently, with rigidly defined ranks among both the secular and the religious orders. Land everywhere belonged ultimately to the state: one of the Dalai Lama's titles was "the great owner." Nobles and Lamas were granted large properties by the Dalai Lama, who personified the state. They enjoyed the right of taxation over the peasants, the right to command their services as cultivators, construction workers, domestic servants, and skilled artisans, on their own estates. The great lords lived in Lhasa, while their estates were taken care of by managers, who bossed the peasants like little kings.[58]

In Lhasa, the nobles performed various kinds of government service. They also "entertained" the people by appearing in rituals and festivals dressed in regalia, color- and quality-graded in accordance with their rank. In matters of costume, at least, the nobles showed that they were sophisticated cosmopolitans, for their robes were decorated with things imported from all parts of the world. Laborers might be ignorant of wheeled vehicles that would have made their lives so much easier, but their superiors showed no such ignorance when their vanity and prestige were at stake. They had their secretaries write to distant countries for this or that article de luxe: blue foxes from Hamburg, pearls from Japan, turquoise from Persia, corals from Italy, and amber from Berlin and Königsberg.[59]

Buddhism is one of the world's great religions—exalted in worldview and doctrine, earthy in practice, as is true of other great religions. The form of Buddhism that eventually took hold in Tibet (Lamaism) includes elements of an older nature cult and of Indian Tantrism, which boasted deities and demons that demanded animal and, in the old days, human sacrifice. Images of fierce demons still glared down from temple walls—a shock to naive visitors who tended to associate Tibetan religion with gentleness and light. This older layer of belief and practice never yielded to the kind of spirituality associated with Buddhism's founder and his greatest followers. Indeed, its role in daily affairs (both religious and secular) was dominant. True, monks could be seen everywhere, and they might be contemplatives, devoted to higher forms of prayer and to acts of impartial kindness, but even more they were magician-healers, oracles, and mediums, and as such they tried to control nearly every aspect of Tibetan life. Monks were jealous of their powers. They resisted competition from modern medicine. Harrer believed that the doctors of the

British legation were the only scientifically trained medical men in the whole country.[60] Monks claimed power not only over the human body but also over the forces of external nature: they could hold up hailstorms or call down rain. Lhasa and many villages had their own weathermakers. In addition to its official weathermaker, Lhasa had six mediums and the state oracle, who looked like an ordinary young man except when he was under a trance and possessed by a god. He would then begin to tremble, beads of sweat stood out on his forehead, his face became swollen and covered with patches of hectic red. "Hissing sounds pierced through his closed teeth. Suddenly he sprang up. Servants rushed to help him, but he slipped by them and to the moaning of the oboes began to rotate in a strange exotic dance. Save for the music, his groans and teeth gnashings were the only sounds to be heard in the temple." When he had quieted down and recovered somewhat, a cabinet minister approached him to elicit his deliverances on war and peace, the appointment of a new governor, the discovery of a new incarnation, and other momentous matters.[61]

Given this somber and rather weird picture of Tibet, the invading armies of communist China, especially after their experiences of welcome in the Chinese countryside, not unreasonably expected a similar reception from Tibetan peasants and serfs. Ordinary Tibetans would indeed have been grateful for land reform and freedom from servitude to the nobles, but the Dalai Lama, responding wisely to the impending invasion, immediately instituted reforms of his own, which removed a major potential source of discontent and undermined China's offer of reform.[62] China also proposed technical innovations to Tibet, and those too were welcome. Many Tibetans quickly saw the value of modern medicine, hospitals, and medical training. They appreciated roads and wheeled vehicles (though not necessarily motorcars), improved agricultural techniques, stockbreeding, irrigation, and forestry. The problem was and is, How far can these processes of modernization and others even more alien to Tibetan tradition (e.g., mining, manufacturing, and tourism) continue without doing irreparable damage to Tibet's identity?

Tibet's dilemma in the second half of the twentieth century takes the form of a number of unresolved conflicts: how to nurture Tibetan nationalism in the shadow of Chinese domination, sustain a religious culture without its superstitions, abandon feudalism without embracing socialism, modernize yet not suffer from its worst effects, and plug into and yet not be overwhelmed by global capitalism. An American journalist, Jeremy Bernstein, visited Tibet in 1987. Like other foreign visitors, he saw many signs of Chinese domination—the presence of strolling soldiers, for example, but he seemed most struck by Tibet's official compliance with Beijing time, which means that "one has to get used to getting up in pitch darkness and going to bed long before sunset."[63] Not long ago, Tibet was a mysterious country sealed off from the world. Suddenly, in the late 1970s and early 1980s, it was thrown open to global capital and modern tourism, with incongruous and even bizarre results. Consider two buildings in Lhasa, each famous in its own way. One is the Potala, which is a huge dormitory for monks, a palace for the living God-king, and a gloomy silent tomb in which the remains of former God-kings are enshrined. The other is the Holiday Inn, which boasts "four hundred and eighty-six twin-bedded guest rooms and suites, each with its own color TV and its own bathroom . . . : two restaurants;

a cocktail lounge with a string quartet whose repertoire includes Mozart and Beethoven."[64]

Lhasa's Jokhang temple provides another vivid example of conflict—this time between Tibetan religiosity and Chinese secularism. The Chinese laid out a mall outside the temple, lined with Soviet-style Friendship stores for tourists. The pilgrims who converged on the temple from all over Tibet turned the mall into a religious park. They prostrated themselves in front of the Jokhang; some crawled around it on their hands and knees, clockwise in accordance with tradition. Crawling around an edifice of power like an animal? The practice is a relic of Oriental despotism and has nothing to do with the spirit, teaching, and example of the Enlightened One. Bernstein witnessed this scene. He also witnessed "pairs of Chinese soldiers, arms linked, walking ostentatiously . . . counterclockwise—the wrong way."[65] The soldiers clearly intended to show disrespect. But disrespect for what? For the Tibetan custom of clockwise pilgrimage or for the crawling? Can these two elements of the ritual be separated? Shouldn't they be? These are some of the questions the Tibetans themselves need to raise if they decide—as they appear to have done with the encouragement of the exiled Dalai Lama—to become more democratic and modern, less entrenched in practices that did not derive from the inspired heart of their religion.

Chinese Cultural Identity

While China continues to assume, even now, cultural superiority over such neighbors as Mongolia and Tibet, in the past one hundred and fifty years it has been forced to confront the inexorably mounting cultural-scientific challenge of the West. Even at the end of the eighteenth century, Chinese mandarins easily brushed off Western superiority in the technical sphere as the mere cleverness of barbarians. By the nineteenth century, such offhand dismissal would have been absurd. China believed at first that it needed to accept only superior Western technology and that primarily in the areas of military hardware and modern manufacturing. Soon it knew that purchased technology was not enough, that it had to learn the fundamentals of Western science. China, even then, hoped to hang on to the superiority of its traditional moral and social order—the Chinese cosmos. Defeat by a modernized Japan in the war of 1894–95 finally forced it to contemplate major overhauls in nearly all areas of culture and life; either that or it could not hope to retain a respected position even in Asia.

Twentieth-century Chinese history is full of epochal events such as the fall of the Manchu dynasty, the establishment of the republic, Japanese invasion, and the communist revolution. Through them all ran, with increasing urgency, the question, What does it mean to be Chinese? The question is not as academic as it sounds, for it is underlain by a profound awareness of China's economic backwardness and poverty, of external threats to nationhood and internal forces that can cause political fragmentation. The Chinese, having for so long equated their own culture with universal culture (civilization), and having taken for granted that other cultures are marginal (local or ethnic), were forced to come to terms with the fact that their own vaunted civilization was just another culture. Moreover, by the nineteenth century, Chinese culture had become so enfeebled that its embers could not be reignited even if the desire had been there.

So the question, raised by intellectuals again and again and answered in a variety of ways, is how to modernize without losing altogether the Chinese essence. The pain of turning to the West was initially cushioned by the desperate belief that China was the original fount of all the technical marvels and political wisdom (including the germinal idea of democracy) that had come to be identified with the West.[66] A far sounder base for confidence building was and is the doctrine that nothing truly good, human, and universal, can be alien to the spirit of Chinese tradition. China cannot be itself unless it feels central, that is, fully at ease in the universe of modern science and in the transcultural ideals of human equality and freedom that are a unique creation of the West. Hu Shih, a leading figure of the Chinese renaissance (the New Culture Movement), asked his countrymen to think of the "new civilization" as of primary importance and Westernization as a secondary matter. Indeed, he preferred to designate the fact of Chinese borrowing from the West not Westernization but "modernization" or "cosmopolitanization."[67]

Some seventy years after Hu Shih, the astrophysicist and democrat Fang Lizhi took up the same idea. He too urged that the Chinese think in temporal rather than spatial terms—that is, use the word "modernization," which suggests an inevitable historical destiny for all humankind, rather than Westernization, or East and West, which tend to bring to mind the idea of fixed levels of achievement—some higher, some lower—in different parts of the world.[68] But not all Chinese intellectuals feel the need for this verbal sleight of hand to salvage their country's self-respect. Some have straightforwardly urged that China abandon its traditions and become part of a global culture. They seem to be saying that the lessons China has been preaching to Tibet and other "marginal" places should be directed at China itself, which, far from being the true "Middle Kingdom," is no less a country of ossified customs, symbols, and beliefs.

One of the most influential of these advocacies for change is a six-part television series called *River Elegy*, which began to appear in the summer of 1988. At last, the intellectuals have found in television a popular and dramatic medium that can reach people far beyond the elite. The basic message is simple: China "must emerge from the constrained, inward focus of 'Yellow River civilization' and head out into the open 'azure ocean civilization.' " In the series, China's great symbols—Yellow River, Great Wall, and Dragon—are all shown to belong to a peasant and authoritarian past. By contrast, the color azure is somehow linked with the progressive forces of science and democracy. More direct and effective is the linking of that color "with the world's billowing oceans, across which explorers such as Ming admiral Zheng He and Western explorers had sought their fortunes."[69] The evocative presentation of a blue frontier, where cultures mix and undergo rebirth, and of red as the color of all people's blood, is intended to show that China's future lies in an outward-directed cosmopolitanism.

What Kind of Cosmopolitanism?

Can this outward-directed cosmopolitanism accommodate elements of traditional Chinese culture, and if so, what will they be? And can these elements be anything other than "song and dance, food, and customs" that the Chinese themselves have promoted at one time—rather condescendingly—to the ethnic minorities? The overall structure of the traditional Chinese cosmos has decayed beyond repair: a striking evidence of it is the near-total demolition of Beijing as a cosmic diagram. (And how extraordinary it is to think that, at the time of the city's takeover by the Red Army in 1949, it was still essentially such a diagram!) Demolition of the old walls had to occur to accommodate a sharp increase in population, but even under socialism commercial and manufacturing activities were on the rise to give the city a quasi-modern appearance.

"Commerce and manufacturing" take us to another meaning of cosmopolitanism. Under this other meaning, a cosmopolite is not someone who lives in an ordered universe but someone who lives in the midst of a rich mixture of peoples, cultures, and goods. As we have noted earlier, these two "cosmoses" are in conflict: universal order sees heterogeneity as ever on the verge of chaos, whereas heterogeneity sees universal order as life-destroying and heavy-handedly authoritarian. The cosmic worldview also cannot accommodate intellectually and ceremonially nonagricultural activities: industry and trade, unlike agriculture, do not swing with the seasons. Within the cosmic city, certain "profane" quarters were reserved for commerce. But we have seen how historically these quarters broke out of their boundaries and spilled into other parts of the city, against governmental wishes. At the national scale, in such periods as the T'ang (618–906) and especially the Southern Sung (1127–1279), the southern cities, which disobeyed nearly all the rules of cosmic planning, prospered commercially, swelled in population (including numerous foreign traders), and became here and there highly cosmopolitan, all in sharp contrast to the foursquare northern cities.[70]

Interestingly, in the late twentieth century, we see emerging a modern parallel to this distinction between North and South, between two kinds of cosmic-cosmopolitan aspiration. Since the 1970s, the dominance of the North and the northern model of cosmos—*t'ien hsia* (all under Heaven)—has been challenged by the South as its economy boomed. The special trade zones, the coastal cities, and rich parts of coastal deltas boast a cosmopolitanism of commerce and manufacturing, a new *t'ien hsia* as it were, with international capital rather than the hieratic sun (emperor and an overarching moral-political ethos) as its centerpiece. To southern intellectuals and foreign observers driven by their own (basically American) ideology of diversity, the South rather than the North is clearly the more dynamic region, culturally as well as economically. But what are the elements of this southern culture? First, it is more democratic and robust, not so much something laid down by government officials, technocrats, and intellectuals, as something that ordinary people can spontaneously want. And what do ordinary people want? They want, after the long drought of marginal living, material—indeed, "luxury"—goods. Increasingly from the 1980s onward, consumer goods of all kinds (many foreign) are embraced as the one demonstrably effective means to liberation. The new culture of the special trade zones and coastal cities is frankly lowbrow and hedonistic. Its egregious components are dubiously Chinese, for they include Disneyland-like entertainment parks, night clubs, and Western-style food marts; on the other hand, there are also the "merry places everywhere" (as a southern university instructor puts it), and it is in these generic "merry places" that a fusion of cultures—Chinese and Western—may occur.[71]

Historically, the dominant movement of Chinese culture and

civilization is from north to south. In the late twentieth century, the tide appears to have turned: a strong current now moves from south to north. This move is both welcomed and abominated by Beijing. Wealth and economic dynamism are welcome, but not the grosser aspects of materialism, the total capitulation before Western styles, the excesses of individualism, the broadening chasm between rich and poor, and, least of all, the prostitution, the violent crimes, the threat of anarchy, the erosion of not only socialist but even communal ideals. At a fundamental level, Beijing's distaste is an aesthetic one that other hierarchical societies also know well: it is the distaste of an elite with its austere vision of cosmic harmony, which may be traditional Chinese, Platonic, puritan-Christian, or socialist, for the people's teeming and proliferating numbers, their inchoate, multifarious, and hungry needs that, freed from constraints once imposed by nature, seem to have no limits. Perhaps the most distasteful aspect of this new culture, from an official and educated-class viewpoint, is the crude mixture of consumerism and resurgent superstitious practices and beliefs, on display most prominently in village funerals.[72]

If consumerism plus superstition represents the nadir of the marriage of modern and traditional, West and East, what would represent the peak? For the past one hundred years, Chinese thinkers have tried to envisage the ideal mixture of elements, with indifferent success. The difficulty begins with the conceptualization itself. Maoism is the most recent heroic effort to apply an overarching Western concept—Marxism-Leninism—to the specific circumstances of China. The result at the end of forty years, notwithstanding certain political and economic gains, is less than inspirational. Its failures may be laid to doctrinaire theory, a rigid

Marxist-Maoist cosmos that allows no deviation, no proliferation of microcosms or hearths in its interstices. In this respect, it is quite unlike the traditional Chinese cosmos, which was able to remain in place for two thousand years, in large part because it was willing to accommodate multiple microcosms in its midst.

The greatest challenge to China today and in the near future is not the maintenance of diversity: in a geographically varied and populous state, diversity tends to emerge on its own as the worldwide resurgence of nationalism and ethnicism shows. Nor is it hearth. The Chinese have a talent for hearth—for small-scale intimacies, for familial warmth and hometown loyalty, for sipping tea and cracking watermelon seeds, talking of stocks and bonds, under the gingko tree. It may be that the hearth in China, as elsewhere, is threatened by the hectic pace, the scale, and the tendency toward uniformity of modernization, but it seems to me that China, given its long and continuous history, is better equipped than many newer nations to resist these pressures. There is, after all, no inherent contradiction between modernization and hearth, and perhaps not even between modernization and diversity, points that I will raise in the concluding chapter.

So what is the biggest challenge to modern China? It is to come up with a powerful image of nationhood that overrides local and regional differences, North and South. Without such an image—without an overarching conception of what China stands for now and in the future—China as a nation-state disintegrates. Here I see a deep paradox. Even if China disintegrates as a nation-state, Chinese civilization—one shared by more than a billion people—will persist for a long time to come: such an enormous mass of deeply ingrained habits cannot simply be wiped out, homogenized in the blender of global modernization. On the other hand, if China succeeds in articulating a national identity it can only be at the expense of its traditional claim to being *t'ien hsia*—all under Heaven. China's historic sense of a collective self lies in not having a national identity—in not being merely one nation among other nations, distinguished from them by the anemic word "difference." The trick for China is to reconstitute or invent a sense of self while discarding all pretensions to superiority and universality that, historically, have been the kernel of that sense of self.

3

THE UNITED STATES

Ethnocentrism is a trait common to all societies. This does not mean, of course, that societies are equally ethnocentric, that they— to anything like equal degree—see themselves not only as the center of the world, a model others naturally look up to, but even as constituting (in all things that matter) the world. To these broad generalizations, I add two more. One is that in premodern times, China was outstandingly ethnocentric, a product of its four thousand years of continuous history in the course of which it encountered only people who were either militarily weaker or culturally less advanced. Contact with the West shattered that view, and we have seen how China has since striven to regain its sense of centrality.

The second generalization is that, in the past two centuries, the United States has been outstandingly ethnocentric, full of confidence in its own superiority, despite the fact that in the early years of its independence it had to acknowledge Europe's far greater military power and cultural wealth. As the year 2000 approaches, the United States retains its sense of centrality. It has been, and is, at the forefront of modernization on both the technological and sociopolitical fronts. Its sense of self is threatened, however, in two major changes during the second half of the twentieth century. One is global modernization—the establishment of a global culture such that no part of it stands out: New York's skyline, at one time the nation's unique signature, is now replicated in many other metropolises. The second change, which no one had predicted before its sudden arrival, is cultural particularism or ethnicity—a movement also strongly manifest in other countries, including (as we have seen) China—that can weaken America's sense of a larger self, with a common past, shared values, and goal.

Conceptions of Centrality and Power

A powerful conception of centrality is the cosmos, built on cardinal points that link the human world to the seasons and hence to the motions of the sun and the stars. China's world picture, elaborated over the centuries, is essentially that. Not so the world picture of the United States and other modern nations. And yet, this is not entirely true. At least in the United States, there is a strong hint of the traditional cosmic schema in the way the country is divided into regions and given directional labels. According to Leslie Fiedler, American writers have always shown an inclination to do that. They have produced literary works that can be justifiably designated Northern, Eastern, Southern, and Western, though, for reasons not immediately clear, only the last is generally called by that name. The Northern is "tight, grey, low-keyed. . . . Typically the scene is domestic, an isolated household in a hostile environment." The landscape is "stern and rock-bound," the weather "deep winter." The Eastern links America with the Old World in a swirl of flirtation and romance. The "season is most appropriately spring, when the ice of New England symbolically breaks and all things seem—for a little while—possible." The Southern is filled with passionate events, sexually driven, set in the "long hot summer," in a countryside of live oaks, miasmal swamp, and decaying plantation house. The Western is confrontation with the Indians, cattle rustlers and other bad guys in a desolate and sweeping landscape. In its most sanitized form, the Western is the cowboy myth of popular fiction and movies in which the lone hero, after saving the homesteaders, rides off into the sunset.[1]

We see here the association of a cardinal region with a particular season: climate, determined by the position of the sun, is integrated into human affairs and passions. This is as close as Americans have come to sharing a cosmic schema that was embraced by people in many other parts of the world. To Americans, however, this schema is only one of several. As I have sketched it here, it reached (perhaps) widest acceptance in the period from the last quarter of the nineteenth to the middle of the twentieth century. Although labeling regions by cardinal points remains a common practice, it now seems to have more political-economic than emotional-evocative significance. The United States moves too fast to be subsumable under a basically static cosmic frame. The intimate links between nature and people, dramatized in the literature of an earlier time, have lost their mythic power as they conform less and less—from the end of World War II onward—to people's actual experience and knowledge. Thus North, rather than evoking deep winter, may call up a pleasing image of summer as New England becomes a resort for tourists; and a modern South, with its air-conditioned cities, is increasingly anachronistic as the stage of lusty passions, played out in the long hot summer of the countryside.

West as Direction and Goal

In America's public consciousness of itself and its place in history, more enduring and more important by far than the static cosmic schema is the dynamic picture of the West as direction and goal.[2] If being situated in the heart of a cosmos can give one a sense of enlargement, being the goal of a vast historical process that begins in remote antiquity can produce a similar—indeed, more inspiring—effect.

How rich are the sources of this myth if one chooses to forage into the past! Ancient Egypt sees the West as the place of the setting sun, whose daily downward path from east to west is from the fertile Nile to the sterile desert, where pyramids guaranteed immortality to the pharaohs. Ancient Greece sees the Isles of the Blest, westward of the Pillars of Hercules, as an idyllic place for the favorites of the gods, or is it for dead heroes? Happiness and immortality lie to the west, but only through the portal of death and desolation—the passage through sterile desert or sea. A melancholic note is discernible in antiquity's dialectic of the West, and this note never quite disappears in the millennial thinking of the modern period. As the sun moves from east to west, so does Christ's message of salvation. Its acceptance in the New World means that the gospel has spread to all four quarters of the earth. To seventeenth-century writers such as Parson Samuel Purchas and Edward Hayes, this accomplishment is followed by the apocalypse, the triumph of the forces of good over evil, and the establishment of the city of God on the earth of the western New World. The sun of Christ, at the end of its progress from east to west, will rise in the West and illuminate the East! As the eighteenth-century divine, Jonathan Edwards, puts it, "The Sun of Righteousness has long been going down from east to west; and probably when the time comes of the church's deliverance from her enemies ... the light will rise in the west, until it shines through the world like the sun in its meridian brightness."[3]

Whereas the millennium is always welcome, the apocalypse—the transition through death—is not. The theological rhetoric of an earlier time seems strange to modern ears. The image of the sun rising from the west is decidedly eschatological: it can only happen when the world as human beings have known it has disappeared. Yet, the idea of a heavenly city at the end of a period of trial is not without resonance in the experience of European immigrants, who must follow the course of the sun, suffer the little deaths of leaving home and the hardships of transit, before reaching the New World and the promise of a new life.

However desirable the goal, leaving home almost always entails some sense of loss: hence the melancholic note in myths of westering. But not by any means in all of them. Indeed, one myth that gained a certain popularity among influential people by late medieval and Renaissance times—Eden at the end of the westward passage—was unshadowed. To explorers and settlers in the sixteenth and seventeenth centuries, west still meant more a direction than a place: it was the direction that led to the fabulous East, and this could be the Cathay of Marco Polo or the garden of the Old Testament, a place that in the words of the cosmographer, Pierre D'Ailly, was "full of pearls and precious stones" and in which people who died centenarians were considered to have died prematurely.

Eden belongs to the beginning of time. Moving westward, if the destination were Eden, meant moving into an innocent past and a pristine place in which wealth, natural fertility, and fountains of youth might all be found. Naturally, this notion could not withstand for long the test of reality: it was soon replaced by a conception of the East that promised merely material wealth. The search for an easy route to Oriental riches, across the barrier of the New World, continued right to the early decades of the Republic.[4] Meanwhile—and indeed even as early as the sixteenth century—the West was becoming a place of exploitable riches in its own right, and not just a direction. The West itself—the New World—became the goal, a goal that signified the future rather than the past.

The fervor of religion gave that future a millennial cast, as we have just noted. But a bright "millennial" future was readily conceivable in secular terms as well. "Westward the course of empire takes its way": this imperial theme of power moving westward has its ancient root in Virgil, who celebrated the rise of Rome, displacing Troy, and its medieval-Renaissance root in Geoffrey of Monmouth, who picked up the Virgilian imperial theme of the West, but transferred that West from Rome to England. In America, the religious and imperial themes conflated. So we see Samuel Sewall declaring in 1713 that America was best suited for "the Government of Christ," precisely because it was "the Beginning of the East, and the End of the West." The New Jerusalem would not emerge from the site of the old Jerusalem, but rather from the farthest West. There, if anywhere, will be built mankind's most holy commonwealth, so Samuel Stillman orated on July 4, 1789.[5]

Throughout the eighteenth and nineteenth centuries, the image of America as the culmination of a sweeping and irresistible historical-geographic process appealed to the nationalistic sentiment of influential citizens. The rhetoric they used varied. They might stress culture rather than religion, as when Nathaniel Ames and Benjamin Franklin saw "Humane Literature (like the Sun) [making progress] from the East to the West," or personal disposition, as when Thoreau admitted as to how the West excited in him an implacable urge. Personal disposition would have mattered little but for the fact that it conformed to and received support from the nation's destiny, which, Thoreau observed, pointed toward Oregon rather than Europe, as in the larger picture mankind itself "progress[ed] from east to west."[6] And then, there was the frankly political-imperial view, which was to culminate in the conception of the United States as possessing a Manifest Destiny.

Nature in America

I am enumerating large ideas, made by men of influence, which for good or ill have given a general cast to American character such that when people of a certain class and educational background compare nations and national traits, they are inclined to say, "Yes, Americans are like that, unlike the French or the Chinese." One such potent idea is that nature—the natural American environment—is a giver of values. Already in the seventeenth century, Puritans who sought to attract their brethren to New England told fantastic tales "of the abundance of crops and game, the magic of the air and water; how life on the new continent cured consumption, gout, and all sorts of fevers; how the old became young, the young became vigorous, and barren women suddenly bore children." In the wilderness, the Puritans went on, the effete would be toughened and the poor enriched by this as yet unexploited paradise. America is the land of the free. How often has this been said by politicians and pamphleteers, in orations, poems, songs, and school texts, as though liberty is bestowed by the very air one breathes and by the very land on which one stands. Turner's frontier hypothesis of 1893 hit a responsive chord in the educated public, surely in part because it was able to capture and give intellectual underpinning to the old and vague presumption that somehow the character of Americans and virtues of their institutions were derived from the land—from people at the frontier owning it, working on it, struggling with it and benefiting ultimately in prosperity and freedom from its natural largesse.[7]

Morals, Americans believe, are safeguarded by nature. Cities corrupt, make people artificial, but so long as nature lies close by, Americans will never lose their natural simplicity and honesty.[8] The new nation lacks cathedrals, but who will miss them so long as there exist the cathedrals of nature—towering peaks and trees—in which moral lessons may be imbibed free of the distortions of books composed by fallible human beings? Perhaps no other belief is so widely shared, so much a part of a general sentiment that goes beyond the book-reading class, since the founding of the republic, although, of course, the particular moral stressed—independence, freedom, manliness, simplicity, an awareness of God's immanence, a posture of modesty commensurate with a profound admiration of nature—varies, as does the language used, which has ranged from philosophical-deistic musings and cool argument to passionate assertions and soaring sermons.

But from the beginning of European contact with the New World, there was also—as Howard Mumford Jones has put it forcefully—the anti-image of nature, one that grew as explorers and settlers recognized that here was no garden, a smiling world of fertile islands, but an immense continent that "stretched to an endless and confusing coastline running from Greenland and Baffin Bay through Gargantuan twistings and turnings to the Strait of Magellan and Tierra del Fuego."[9] Whatever the expectations, direct experience of wilderness often provoked bewilderment and horror. This was the response of Pilgrims at Plymouth harbor and it was the response repeatedly of explorers, travelers, and settlers who have moved to the frontier. What was one to make of the vastness, the turbulence, the violence, and even the disconcerting plenitude of nature? Of the Missouri River, Francis Parkman wrote:

> Born among mountains, trackless even now [1870] . . . it holds its angry course through sun-scorched deserts, among towers and palaces, the architecture of no human hand, among lodges of barbarian hordes, and herds of bison blackening the prairies to the horizon. Fierce, reckless, headstrong, exulting in its tumultuous force, it plays a thousand freaks of wanton power; bearing away forests from its shores, and planting them, with roots uppermost, in its quicksands.[10]

And this, according to Howard Mumford Jones, was the sort of impression formed by John James Audubon, Edmund Flagg, Basil Hall, Mrs. Trollope, Thomas Nuttall, Charles A. Murray, Captain Marryat, Alexander Mackay, and innumerable other travelers.

The Idea of Progress

The idea of progress is without doubt one of the reigning ideas in this country. Americans in the past and even now have generally found it plausible, despite mounting criticism. Why? One factor may well be the myth of the movement of true religion and civilization from east to west, culminating in North America: geographical progress—progress in the old sense of stately motion has taken on the newer, temporal sense of improvement. But the impact of this myth could not have extended much beyond the literate class. A more important factor is simply the experience of the immigrants. Although the vast majority of them are unlikely to have entertained progress as an intellectual idea—a theory of history and evolution—their experience in America has nevertheless confirmed it. They have come to this country to better their lives, and they—and if not they, then their children—have by and large succeeded in doing so.

The third factor is a combination of direct experience and belief—the experience of an intractable nature and the belief that human beings can tame it by introducing a progressive succession of improvements. Intractable nature was perceived as primordial nature. Such a view put the New World into the past rather than into the future. In crossing the Atlantic, one had arrived at an older world, representing the childhood of humankind. European explorers and settlers took for granted that the native inhabitants of North America were savages, just as they regarded the natural environment as savage; and both were to be steadily raised to civilized standards, which were assumed to be those of Europe. Civility and civilized behavior in Europe, as Norbert Elias has reminded us, gained notably in importance in the sixteenth century, when, for instance, certain books on etiquette (outstandingly that by Erasmus) became popular. Europeans were becoming historically conscious, if only in the crude sense of believing that they had moved from an unmannerly past into a mannerly present, and that improvements in personal appearance and behavior were paralleled by a similar upgrading of the material environment.[11]

During the colonial period and in the early years of independence, Americans were inclined to accept Europe's theory of cultural evolution, but when they did so they found themselves in an awkward position, for while their culture (from their perspective) was a couple of notches above that of the Indians, it did not measure up to European culture. Colonial Americans were aware of the crudeness of their dwellings and farms—their manner of life in general—but felt confident that soon their world would be more like that of cultured Englishmen. On the other hand, they—especially after independence—could boast that their simple manners, good government, and modestly humanized landscapes were a sort of golden mean between the primitiveness of the Indians and the decadent worldliness of the Europeans. In the grossly biased view of the time, the natives of North America were savages, but compared with the European poor, "Every Indian was a gentleman," said Benjamin Franklin. The worth of the golden mean was implied by the physician William Currie when he wrote in 1792 that North America deserves praise, because it is "the only portion of this spacious globe where man can live securely, and enjoy all the privileges to which he has a native right. In this enviable and favored region there is no proud usurping aristocracy, no ecclesiastical orders with exclusive privileges, no kings with arbitrary power. . . . None of the enervating refinement of luxury or dissipation are to be found here; but here all the necessaries and conveniences of life abound, and a pleasing equality and decent competence are everywhere displayed."[12]

We have in this passage—and there were many passages of this kind in the utterances and writings of Americans in the second half of the eighteenth century—a juxtaposition of boastfulness and modesty. On the one hand, there was the hyperbole that America was the "only portion of this spacious globe" where certain essentials of the good life could be found; on the other hand, these essentials were themselves modest—not luxuries and enervating refinements, but "necessaries and conveniences," not pomp and privilege, not (perhaps) even genius, but "pleasing equality and decent competence." As we contemplate America two hundred years later, many could wish that the nation was content to stop at the point where it had been able to offer necessaries and conveniences rather than a superfluity of goods, where its greatest boast was pleasing equality and the competence to make decent houses and farms rather than Faustian will and the unbounded ability to extend and conquer—build transcontinental railroads and superhighways, skyscrapers and spacecrafts, and so create in time an industrial-technological society that, for all its success in bestowing material benefits to a wide segment of the population, has been unable to diminish economic inequality and might even have broadened it; a society that in its greed, in its belief in the inexhaustible plenitude of nature ("herds of bison blackening the prairies to the horizon"), has done great damage to its habitat.

Enlightenment—Uniformity and Abstraction

The United States of America was born in the Age of Reason, a time of optimism and confidence, of the belief that the childhood of mankind, with its superstitions and ignorant passions, has been left behind, and that a bright future is no longer a pipe dream or illusion but well within the possibility of human attainment. One sign of that confidence, at the level of thought, is the habit of talking about human nature and society abstractly, in terms of fundamental principles and truths, inspired in part by the earlier successes in using that sort of language in natural philosophy. No matter how often the opening words of the Declaration of Independence are said, their austere elegance and simplicity—almost mathematically direct—continue to command admiration. "We hold these truths to be self-evident . . ." *We* hold, not some of us or even most of us. The truths are self-evident. Self-evident to what or whom? Self-evident to reason—to the proper exercise of reason, which is within the power of all human beings in sound body and mind.

The federal Constitution, that other great document of American nationhood, doesn't open with quite the force and eloquence of the Declaration, but its prefatory words are nonetheless gripping in succinctness and self-confidence. "We the people of the United States . . . do ordain and establish . . . " We the people—not even people in the plural, which could suggest division and differences of opinion. The all-too-human sources of the Constitution, the unavoidable bickerings and compromises, are hidden in the final wording, which implies that the fundamental principles of government are inherent to the nature of things, and hence not to be considered a mere construct of the time. The Constitution stresses checks and balances within a general conception of order, and that was how nature itself appeared to the framers: nature was a matter of forces and countervailing forces, of "checks and balances," which in sum worked toward the har-

mony of the whole. The Constitution was intended to be for all
time, and it is amazing how few amendments (compared to state
constitutions) have been added to it, and how civic Americans—and not only legal experts—continue to refer to the Constitution, debate its wording and meaning, as though it were a
contemporary document.

The framers of the Constitution intended it to guide the future,
and they saw that the best way to do so was not to fence it in. The
document is self-denyingly brief—only twenty-five pages long, in
contrast to some state constitutions, which can be very verbose. The
shortness—this lack of detailed specification—allows for interpretation and expansion to accommodate changing circumstances. Indeed, the framers provided the formal means to amend the Constitution. However, to give the document weight and stability, they also
made amendment a rather difficult process; more difficult, in fact,
than "amending" the nation (as Boorstin) puts it. The nation can be
amended, that is added to, state after state, by a simple majority vote
in Congress. The states thus created, as well as the original thirteen,
were all considered "equal" despite striking differences in population, resources, and stage of development. They were all designed to
be alike in basic governmental institutions and procedures. Yet,
within this framework, all kinds of adjustments could be made to
suit the needs of the people settling the frontiers, in different climes
and under different conditions. The development of a hierarchy of
states was forestalled—the sense of a "mother country" (or core)
supervising and dominating the "colonies" avoided; so successful
was this equalization, in fact, that within a short period of time the
western "colonies" were able to dominate the politics of the Eastern
seaboard.[13]

What I wish to emphasize here is the working out of an abstract ideal embodied in the Constitution. The way the nation expanded and the speed at which it expanded went against the grain of slower, "natural" processes by which, historically, centers have so often been able to rule, patronize, develop, and exploit the margins. The framers of the Constitution gave weight to the margins—the frontier states—by intellectual fiat. One result is a certain uniformity across a political landscape of continental size.

Abstract thinking frequently results in constructions that are visibly artificial. The states have not grown in an organic fashion. Their shape is more or less rectangular, with (often) straight lines that defy topography. Americans have come to take the artificial shape of their state for granted. Geometric order in the landscape is a common experience for many people. The cause of this common experience lies not, of course, in the straight state borders, which are conspicuous only on maps, but in the U.S. land survey and in the grid pattern of many towns and cities. The townships of the land survey, each bounded by east-west and north-south lines, each thirty-six miles in area, and systematically subdivided to the smallest unit—the "forty"—were designed in the 1780s, adopted in 1785, and eventually applied to most parts of the Western states and the Mississippi basin. In practice, numerous compromises had to be made with topography. Nevertheless, the rectangular pattern has become a distinctive feature of the American landscape, especially when viewed from the air, but the pattern can also be experienced on the ground, as when one drives along a country road and is repeatedly forced to make right-angle turns.

The township-and-range survey represents a major departure from the traditional "metes and bounds" measures that were applied to the Eastern seaboard—measures that make no fetish of precision and take advantage of natural and constructed landmarks. The new survey may be considered a product of the Enlightenment—a way of thinking that values rationality, proportion, and orderly process. Social harmony itself was and is believed to be a fruit of rationality, of "order on the land." Who knows but that the rectilinearity (the rectitude, as it were) of the survey has contributed to public peace, and that the Wild West would have been even more anarchic without its defining power—its sobering lucidity?[14]

The grid pattern of towns and cities facilitated the sale of property. Crass materialism, rather than any sort of geometric ideal, motivated its widespread adoption. Yet, there is no denying that it also promoted orderly process and efficiency of settlement and, moreover, projected an air of welcoming openness to strangers. A grid town is quickly known—a fact appreciated by people passing through. By the same token, it could quickly seem monotonous. American towns have often been criticized for their lack of individuality and picturesqueness. There is not only the uniformity of the street pattern, there is also the sameness of "brick buildings along main street and freestanding frame houses, each with a lawn," along the perpendicular side streets. One town is much like another. Rather than humdrum sameness, however, J. B. Jackson suggests that what American towns show is conformity to a distinctive American style. "Classical is the word for it. . . . Rhythmic repetition (not to say occasional monotony) is a Classical trait, the consequence of devotion to clarity and order."[15]

A lack of differentiation has frequently been leveled at the man-made American landscape, from the early years of independence to our own time, by foreigners as well as natives. In the early 1800s, certain Americans, sensing a deficiency of splendor and variety in their land, yearned for the vivid contrasts to be found in Europe—between (say) London and Paris, Berlin and Naples, country house and peasant cottage, cathedral and parish church. Alexis de Tocqueville, for all his admiration of democracy, confessed that "the sight of such universal uniformity saddens and chills me." A question that needs to be raised at this point is, Was America all that uniform? Uniformity could well have resulted from selective vision—from not looking at certain peoples and places, for example, slave quarters, Indian clearings, and differences in immigrant architectural and living style that should have been evident to the observer even during the late colonial period.

Europe's landscape would be much duller if there were not an established and enforced hierarchy—if there were no lords and peasants, merchants of great wealth and ordinary traders.[16] Compared with Europe, citizens in colonial and early-nineteenth-century America belonged to more or less the same class. This narrowed social range was a factor in creating an appearance of "sameness" among the farmsteads, villages, and townships in the northern tier of states. America's political institutions were designed to discourage the emergence of great disparities of power and status. In a democracy, a measure of "uniformity" might well be considered desirable in itself. Nevertheless, even as a distant ideal, America did not seriously aspire to become a republic of letters as the Enlightenment thinkers had envisaged it, that is, a cosmopolitan society of well-educated citizens contributing equally to discourses concerning the public good. That would have run aground on ethnoreligious diversity; moreover, it would have called for sacrifices in the private pursuit of happiness on one's own farm, in one's own community, which lay historically closer to the American dream. On the other hand, equality was and remains important to Americans, to be striven for, even if the cost were to make buildings and neighborhoods, people and places, look alike. To a remarkable degree, this equality was actually attained, though perhaps less by direct and forceful political action than by (from the late nineteenth century onward) the successes of the technologies of mass production and mass distribution—the rational organization of the material world that might itself be seen as a fulfillment of the Enlightenment program. This is, of course, a familiar story: middle Americans, for all their differences in income, level of education, ethnic background and religious belief, have become "one," thanks to the day-to-day experience of using the same sorts of household tools, living in the same sorts of houses, shopping in the same sorts of general stores or supermarkets, eating the same packaged and franchised foods, watching the same sports, and seeing the same shows. An American abroad may feel homesick for Storrs, Connecticut, that is, a specific place; on the other hand, he could well also feel homesick for something that can be found just about anywhere in the sprawling country.[17]

Enlightenment and Revivalism—Reason and Passion

Enlightenment ideals have affected the American nation at birth. But what were these ideals? Not components that added up to a harmonious whole, for they, and the driving forces (the temperaments and motivations) behind them, were often incompatible. Henry May, in *The Enlightenment in America*, recognizes three kinds of Enlightenment—skeptical, moderate, and revolutionary. Skeptical enlightenment, which is grounded in the free use of corrosive reason, has never been important except to a small elite in this country. How could it be? How could any social experiment, much less the founding of a whole new nation, be ventured in the teeth of unrelenting skepticism? Enlightenment of both the moderate and revolutionary kind, by contrast, played important roles in the late colonial and early independence era. Moderate enlightenment was embraced by the prosperous and the well educated. Calvinist in the North and Anglican in the South, their basic values were much the same—balance, order, rationality. Most of the framers of the constitutions were of the moderate persuasion. Government, they saw, "must be framed to fit our mixed nature, in which reason and passion, public spirit and lust for power balance each other much as the orbits of the planets are controlled by the forces of mutual attraction and repulsion. Its primary purpose is to protect liberty, and liberty includes control of one's own property as well as one's person."[18]

Revolutionary enlightenment, represented in America by such eminences as Paine and Jefferson, saw the turmoils of their time as the birth pangs of a new age that would leave behind forever the wickedness and folly of ancient ideas and institutions. There was more than a touch of religious enthusiasm in their rhetoric. Paine, indeed, used the vocabulary of biblical millennialism: "We have it in our power to begin the world over again. A situation similar to the present has not happened since the days of Noah until now."[19]

Religion, whether the emphasis was on God the guarantor of order or on God the creator, found a comfortable niche in the presentations of both moderate and revolutionary enlighten-ments. But the religion thus presented and enacted was far too cool and formal for many people. Among the dissenters might be a religious genius like Jonathan Edwards, whose God was an un-knowable ruler, with the absolute right to do whatever he pleased, rather than the maintainer of a predictable cosmos. But mostly they were people with less education, less prosperity, people at the margins of society, including new immigrants exposed to Wes-leyan and Jansenist views at home, who were driven by their strong feelings, fueled in part by their resentment of the elite's calm air of superiority, to express their faith theatrically, with much falling, shouting, loud singing, and speaking in tongues.

There could be no real contest between the measured doctrines of the older churches (Congregational, Anglican, Lutheran, Pres-byterian) and the fervors of revivalism associated with the newer ones (Methodist, Baptist, Separatist). Passion always had the up-per hand over reason, for passion had the people on its side. Re-vivalism periodically swept the country, like "wild fire," as the saying goes. The first revival, known as the Great Awakening, oc-curred in the 1740s and 1750s, the second at the turn of the cen-tury and continued for the next two decades, leading to the third, which culminated in the years before the outbreak of the Civil War. And, of course, revivals remain a recurrent feature of the twentieth century, including those led by the Billy Grahams and Oral Robertses of our day.

One can always distinguish, in a generalized way, between re-ligion's emotionalism and reason's calm. In America, however, the distinction was blurred by the fact, already noted, that mod-erate enlightenment did not dissociate itself from religion, and that revolutionary enlightenment, with its millennial hope and fervor, carried religious overtones in rhetoric if not in doctrine. Distaste for revivalism was limited to an Eastern elite, which made it all the easier to dismiss by people at large. Indeed, revivals in time came to be seen as quintessentially American. To its leaders, the rebirth of faith providentially played a role in taming frontier wilderness, substituting godly sobriety and order for anarchy, drunkenness, and degeneration into heathenism. It signified the ability of the different branches of Protestant Christianity to cooperate and move toward the common goal of implanting the Message of Hope on the frontier West and, as a sort of backwash, rejuvenating religion in the East, which succumbed all too readily to metaphysical sophistry (endless debates about First Cause) and worldliness. The world itself, beyond the borders of the United States, was a missionary field. It is clear that the ideals, images, and rhetoric of the nineteenth-century revivals dovetailed into those of the myth of the West and, on a political plane, those of Manifest Destiny.[20] The moralism that has been an ingredient of American character since the beginning was not allowed to die, its embers being periodically reinflamed by ardent evangelism. America, even in the twentieth century, can see itself as a "City upon the Hill"—the last best hope of humankind.

Moderate enlightenment is embodied in the Constitution—in the forms and procedures, the checks and balances, of federal and state government. And so at least one thrust of the Enlightenment (the moderate English and Scottish kind) continues to affect, directly and indirectly, the lives of most Americans. On the other hand, both skeptical reason and formal analytical reason were and still are suspect. Skepticism is incompatible with optimism, formal reason with enthusiasm for radical change. Somehow people must have felt, even without the benefit of specialized education, that a harmonious cosmos of the ancient Greek or Chinese (i.e., traditional) variety, or even of Newton's variety, did not suit the dynamism of a new nation that was constantly on the move. Revivalism was anti-intellectual, even antieducation. Revivalists and missionaries of the nineteenth century attributed the decline of earlier civilizations to their excessive dependence on the intellect. American civilization would not suffer a similar fate. Yet revivalists were not technological primitivists. They did not despise the useful products of scientific thinking. Indeed, missionaries saw the coming of steam and electricity as part of the same radical change for the better that they so vigorously promoted in the religious sphere.[21] In this sketch of the revivalist, it is possible to discern also the stereotypical image of the white secular male (not altogether false even if it is a stereotype)—someone loudly optimistic, a booster for America, anti-intellectual, yet a ready consumer of technology.

American Enlightenment: Two Dark Events

Great ideals and stories—fervent beliefs—have power. There could not be a United States of America without them. It is in the nature of ideals to move ahead of reality, and of stories that inspire to depict in broad strokes, missing significant details, highlighting features that please and repressing those that are problematic. The older history textbooks, as modern scholars like to point out, have either skimped or grossly distorted two dark events—the removal or killing of Amerindians and the enslavement of Africans.

Enlightenment views played a role in both events, though at times in subtle and indirect ways. Consider, for instance, the idea of progress. It predated the Enlightenment but found its most confident expression then. Progress was believed to have occurred in different areas of life. In the cultural area, commentators typically described the move up as from primitiveness to refinement. European settlers, as one might predict, put Indians at the lower end and themselves at the upper end of the curve. Indian resistance to Europeanization was baffling to well-disposed whites, whereas to the ill-disposed, it simply confirmed their view that the natives were subhuman, part of the rawness and savagery they knew from their encounters with nature. And so, just as the fearsome forests were to be cleared, wolves driven out or eradicated, so Indians were to be removed or exterminated, leaving room for Europeans to introduce and develop the higher stages of culture. Riding roughshod over the natives was also facilitated by the view that there were not many of them. The rhetoric of making a fresh start—of turning a new page—encouraged the perception of America as virgin land inhabited at most by "some tribes of naked and miserable savages."[22]

The other severe blight on the new nation was slavery. Slaves increased in British America by more than 200 percent between 1740 and 1770, much more rapidly than did whites. Southern aristocrats, well educated and well aware of the stirs of liberation in Europe, detested the institution; yet they were either unwilling or felt helpless to change it. Enlightenment among the more sophisticated members of the Southern upper class was generally of the skeptical sort. The presence of an irrational institution in their midst made them give up any attempt to explain God's unfathomable ways or those of men. They indulged, as May puts it, in "few utopian hopes for humanity but valued wit, courage, and intellectual honesty." To their credit, late-colonial plantation owners did not argue that slaves benefited from their condition, as did their nineteenth-century successors.[23]

Intellectual honesty meant an ability to face facts. How frequently leaders of opinion in the Age of Reason on both sides of the ocean failed to do so! The founding of the American Republic raised high hopes for human progress. In the euphoria, patriots were only too prone to forget their society's dark underpinnings. The same forgetfulness could afflict European philosophers. Condorcet, for example, was able to dismiss African bondage in his praise of the wonders of equality in the United States.[24] The new nation did have shining achievements to show, which, in the generally optimistic mood of the time, could be blinding. In sober moments, however, Europeans were well aware of slavery's existence, and they condemned it with increasing fervor in the late decades of the eighteenth century. In doing so they showed themselves more radical than the framers of the Constitution. To keep slaves was, for the philosophers, un-European and uncivilized. By that criterion, the United States, in its desire to be refined and civilized, had a long way to go.[25]

Harmonious Whole versus Diversity

Which has greater appeal, harmonious whole or diversity? In Enlightenment Europe, Newton and Buffon anchored these two poles. Newton stood for simplicity and harmony: nature, if one looked primarily to the heavens, could be understood under a few elegant laws. Buffon, by contrast, was a naturalist whose eyes were turned to the ground, there to discover an amazing plenitude of being. If the stars in their majestic motion reflected God's austere aestheticism, the swarms of plants and animals on earth reflected God's fecundity. Both were admirable in their way, but it was rare that the same persons could admire both equally. Nature images and political ideals were curiously wedded to one another, suggesting that they had roots in the same emotional-aesthetic drive. A tendency toward conservatism went with a preference for Newton's universe, the outstanding virtues of which were simplicity, order, and a certain moral-intellectual seriousness. By contrast, a tendency toward liberalism went with an appreciation for Buffon's world of pullulating plants and animals—with his nature studies: their virtues were a sense of wonder, free-floating imagination, delight in the new and the strange, a playful—even frivolous—spirit.

Around 1800, when the character of the new United States was being formed and debated, Federalists and Republicans disagreed with one another vehemently. The disagreements, though political, spilled to different conceptions on the proper study of nature. Federalists favored astronomy, Republicans natural history. Federalists, with their intellectual stronghold in Boston's Academy of Arts and Sciences and their political base in New England, favored astronomy in part because it was the science of the *Principia*. For them, mathematics had an appeal analogous to the appeal of republican Rome: both projected an aura of probity, austerity, and universality. Federalists viewed Republican science—the science of the Southerners—as mere gentlemanly interest in the plants and animals that could be found on their farms. Significantly, Benjamin Franklin did not even include astronomy in his original prospectus for the American Philosophical Society, an institution that tended to align itself, intellectually, with the South. To Federalists, the mathematical sciences (astronomy, par excellence) required a disciplined and contemplative frame of mind, whereas the descriptive sciences favored by their rivals (botany, geology, and paleontology) catered to curiosity—and curiosity, with its hint of vulgarity, was not then a good word. Why did the Federalists object to the Louisiana Purchase? A prime reason was political: additions of territory to the South would weaken New Englanders in the politics of balance. But there was also the reason that, to Federalists, the West was a land of marvels, a weird country that would whip up even more the appetite of natural historians for self-indulgent investigation.[26]

Both Federalists and Republicans (Jeffersonians) recognized that a properly educated citizenry was essential to the maintenance and prosperity of the Republic. All responsible and thinking men feared the mob. How best to channel the populace's energies and refine their instincts was a constant worry and source of disagreement. Federalists, with their suspicion of human nature dating back to Puritan roots, stressed the need to discipline the mind and the passions through an exposure to the classics and the mathematical sciences. By contrast, Jeffersonians, more optimistic about human nature and more inclined to see curiosity in a favorable light, were ready to believe that nature's fecundity and diversity could offer delight rather than diversion, provide opportunities for exercising the intellect rather than for its entanglement in trivia, leading to a downfall.[27]

Diversity can be an attribute of natural things, but also of things that people have transformed to varying degree; and diversity can of course be an attribute of the human population. Consider, first, things. A traditional potentate, we have noted elsewhere, may seek to affirm his standing as world ruler by gathering exotic plants and animals from distant parts and bringing them to his capital. Jefferson was not a potentate, and he did not seek his own glory. But he did seek prosperity and perhaps even a certain measure of glory for his country, and one way to achieve them was to remake the environment. He experimented with figs from France and rice from Africa and Italy; he learned cheesemaking from Lombardy peasants and sought to introduce the olive tree to Virginia. He was successful in bringing over the merino sheep and the Algerian bantam, but failed, despite repeated tries, to domesticate the nightingale. "Discussing the possibility of introducing the breadfruit tree . . . he wrote that 'one service of this kind rendered to a nation is worth more than all the victories of the most splendid pages of their history.' "[28]

One cannot help but think that Jefferson had an exuberance that his critics, the Federalists, lacked. The more extreme Federalists of New England, who included among them the high clergy, were suspicious of the French, the Irish, and other aliens already on America's shores. Sincerely antislavery, they nevertheless painted lurid pictures of French-led Santo Domingo blacks invading the South. Federalists believed in the Enlightenment, but in their suspicion of human nature and fear of anarchy they tended to withdraw to an elitist and protected world of their own that was the opposite of cosmopolitan.[29] This besieged mentality could offer no inspiration to a new nation founded on human possibility, a nation that, moreover, was settled by different peoples from the start. Contrast this mentality with the delight in the diversity of nature and of humankind that was an outstanding characteristic of Jefferson. "As the creator has made no two faces alike, so no two minds, and probably no two creeds." He meant this as a compliment to God. To Jefferson, the study of the variety of creation was itself an act of worship.[30]

American ambivalence toward diversity in people and culture goes back to colonial times and remains today a lively issue. Diversity provoked and still provokes a mixture of pride and anxiety. In colonial British America, an Englishman would not be exposed to the barely comprehensible dialects he readily found at home, but he would hear foreign tongues far more often. "So generous a man as Franklin," writes May, "worried lest Pennsylvania become Germanized; travelers to Albany reported with irritation that one could not converse without knowing Dutch. Already stereotypes existed: Germans were dull-witted, the Dutch tight-fisted, the French frivolous, the Irish . . . hard-drinking and ignorant."[31]

Diversity was welcome if it added color and zest to cosmopolitan life, but not if it caused mutual incomprehension and antagonism. Diversity was welcome if it enriched conversation, introduced new ways of thinking, but not if it led to a Tower of Babel. Diversity was welcome if it did not throw into doubt the fundamental agreement on what it meant to be an American. Diversity, in short, was welcome if it was superficial, a surface play that entertained, or a temporary phenomenon that fed into and enhanced the common life. And this feeding into the common life is, of course, what *E pluribus unum* means—"from many to one."

The ever-shifting goal is this "oneness" or unity, the existence of which would make the word "American" more than just the label for an arbitrary congery of characteristics.

But if one were to persist and ask, "Just what adds up to being an American?" the answer tends to be a stereotype, or a small number of traits that do not reflect the richness of the component cultures and peoples. Historically, the praise of diversity seemed halfhearted because diversity was so commonly treated as a mere halfway house to something better—a composite Americanness to which all immigrants could aspire. Consider the views of St. John de Crèvecoeur. That "strange mixture of blood" (English, Scotch, Irish, French, Dutch, German, and Swedish) he found in America and nowhere else was clearly a cause for wonder. He called the mixing "promiscuous," not exactly an encomium, and yet the result was a people of whom he approved. Different "races," he believed, could live together because all sought to escape from want and poverty, and all aspired to "the enjoyment of plenty and affluence." And in this dedication to economic betterment, all tended to "think more of the affairs of this world than those of the next." An indifference to religion would displace the sectarian zeal that once divided people, and Crèvecoeur regarded this indifference as "one of the strongest characteristics of the Americans."[32]

There we have it: an original inchoate richness of cultures and beliefs reduced to a negative commonality of religious indifference. But was there really this indifference, this degree of secularization? In the search for economic success, Americans might indeed allow their religious faith to cool, but Christian faith was something that, apparently, could be revived in America. Religious fervor swept the country with the predictability of long-range weather cycles. What did become diluted in successful revivalism was sectarian diversity and strife. Again and again, sectarian differences were submerged in the full tide of a resurgent faith. An outstanding example is the Cane Ridge (Kentucky) revival of 1801. Although it fragmented the Presbyterian Church, it nevertheless came to be regarded as a mighty symbol of concordance, for there, as Perry Miller puts it, "Presbyterians, Methodists, Baptists mingled as one Christian people, and fell in windrows before whichever sort of preacher could slay them."[33]

We can now see certain contradictions in revivalist rhetoric. Preachers were vehemently against the idea of a state church, which to them meant top-down authority and doctrinal orthodoxy. They favored instead a diversity of organizations, but the reason for favoring it was the belief that somehow it actually promoted a spirit of communion. And while a state church was un-American, revivalism, by cutting across denominations, was peculiarly American—the spirit that not only saved souls but unified the nation.[34]

Diversity of peoples, coming from different backgrounds and faiths, is a fact of life in the land of immigrants. What holds them together? What are their common experiences and values? Various answers have been given, including the answer that what unifies them is a kind of generalized religious faith—the "In God We Trust" on American coins. Revivalists have no doubt hoped for something more fervent and more specifically Christian than that, but, in our time of increasing diversity and fragmentation, they are unlikely to get their wish. To return to the question of what unifies Americans, two answers—two kinds of experiences and values—appear to have enjoyed fairly wide and consistent support. One is the image of America as a "golden land," a term often used by the immigrants themselves.[35] Under that rather blatantly materialistic notion is hidden (if one is motivated to search) a cluster of higher values, including freedom, opportunity, and hope. The other answer is the inherited democratic practices and institutions of basically British origin. Ethnic organizations may differ in purpose and goal, yet their views on what constitutes proper procedure in conducting business (voting, majority rule, etc.) tend to be alike. In short, they are unified in their public personae and as citizens.[36]

These answers are problematic for various reasons, two of which stand out. One is the objection that Native Americans and African Americans have not come to this country as immigrants seeking betterment in their lives. Moreover, compared with European and Asian groups who did come as immigrants, they have benefited least, in modern times, from the country's resources and opportunities. To most Native Americans and African Americans, America—the modern United States—has not turned out to be the golden land. Indeed, none of the overarching myths I have sketched earlier—the West, progress, the timeless wisdom of the founding documents, and the golden land—seem to apply to them. The second objection, or difficulty, strikes a chord in perhaps all Americans: it is that what holds them together seems so impersonal. Neither economic success nor the dignified procedures of citizenship offer deep emotional reward. America, so large and diverse, cannot be readily embraced as homeland or patrie, with a catch in the throat. The very name—the United States of America—says nothing very specific. It is not, for instance, the name of a people as is France, Germany, or Thailand. And the more Americans participate in, and indeed lead the world, in globalism, the more they yearn for locality, tradition, and roots—for the hearths and ethnos that they can directly experience and understand, for the small milieu that yields emotional satisfaction.

Hearths

The United States of America, this powerful political unit (cosmos) of continental size, could not have come into being and probably cannot continue to exist without underpinning by overarching ideas, myths, or (to use a currently popular term) metanarratives of rhetorical power. Their story lines have differed in detail, of course, and might even be contradictory at points, but they all tended to suggest some kind of movement, enlargement, and openness; they evoked space and a generous nature, opportunity and freedom, frontier and Manifest Destiny, and democracy itself as a shining goal rather than as a state that had already been achieved. Yet, from the start of the European settlement of North America, there had also been aspirations and supporting myths that were the opposite of these grand visions, stressing instead the virtues and delights of a simplified and smaller world. Europe was the cosmos—a sophisticated but also corrupt civilization; by contrast, the New World, with its isolating and protective spaces, was where the human yearning for true community could once again take hold.

Early English colonies subsequent to the one established in Virginia were almost all experiments in utopian living—efforts to reintroduce a purer (which sometimes meant an earlier) way of life.

Thus, in Maryland, Lord Baltimore hoped to found a well-ordered feudal society as a refuge for his Catholic coreligionists. In a New York reclaimed from the Dutch (1664), the proprietor (the future James II) sought to implement an absolutist regime modeled after the one Louis XIV was establishing in France. In Pennsylvania, William Penn envisaged an ideal community of balanced government and religious tolerance. Humanitarians in the 1730s sought to set up a benevolent colony in Georgia that was to be composed of small independent landowners and free of slavery. None of these undertakings succeeded. The one exception was, of course, the attempt by the English Puritans to set up a community of God's chosen people in Massachusetts.[37]

Small utopian communities have always been and remain a common feature of the American social-cultural landscape. Few of them could endure for more than a few years. Those that did invariably had the backing of religion. The Amish are a famous example. And it is worth recapturing some of that people's characteristic traits, for they so vividly point to the rewards of exclusivity. One reward is identity. The Amish, in sharp contrast to rootless urbanites, have the strongest possible sense of who they are. Everything in their daily lives—dress, food, shelter, language, and religious practice—sets them apart from the larger society and enforces their sense of self. Another reward is stability. The Amish refuse to be drawn into the modern world's maddening pace of change: their picturesque horse-drawn buggies are an example of their desire to slow down and to live close to the earth. With the slower pace is the reward of calm, a calm that is ultimately grounded in religious faith. The Amish enjoy warm familial and communal relationships, sustained by the needs of household management, cooperative farming, and the many participatory rituals of religion. Helpfulness is always expected and valued, and its test is action, not speech. Politeness is eschewed as socially pretentious, and used primarily in encounters with strangers.[38]

The world of the Amish, though small, is not necessarily narrow or constraining. A landscape of neat and variegated farms is their largest handiwork, and as with any significant handiwork or art it can feed the spirit. Moreover, the Amish do not in any sense see themselves as located at the margins of the cosmos, shunted into the side channels of human venture and destiny. To the contrary, in a nonaggressive way they see themselves as "a chosen people of God."

Historically, immigrants came to America to escape religious-political oppression and to seek better economic opportunity. They expected life chances to open up for them in the New World. This "opening up" might be more psychological than physical, however; that is, perceived more as the freedom to establish a known and beloved way of life, at risk in the Old Country, than as taking up space at the frontier or experimenting with newer ways of thinking and living. The New World, in short, offered scope for conservatism. German immigrants provide an outstanding illustration of this attitude. They did not come to be Americanized; rather they came in the hope of setting up new Germanys (i.e., scattered German colonies). They insisted on retaining their own customs and language, which they considered superior to those of the Yankee Puritans. And in this effort they were remarkably successful, until World War I. Take Hermann, Missouri, for example. Incorporated in 1835, the settlers soon persuaded the Missouri state legislature to declare that their school "shall be and forever remain a German school, in which all branches of science and education shall be taught in the German language." A man visiting Hermann and its countryside in 1845 gave his impression that while there "one forgets that one is not actually in Germany itself." As late as 1907, German was the language most often heard on the streets and in businesses.[39]

The attitude of the German Americans toward their adopted country was curiously ambivalent throughout the latter part of the nineteenth century. On the one hand, as we have noted, they wished to retain German culture—a *gemütlich* world of music societies and beer gardens. On the other hand, they recognized from the beginning that they could do so because they were in the land of the free. There was, then, an awareness of this larger, accommodating world. A certain commitment to it would seem fitting. One indication of such commitment lies in the census of 1910, which shows that the German-born group was more prone to become naturalized than was any other foreign group. Clearly, German immigrants were not all equally attached to custom and tradition. The general rule was the better the education, the less the attachment. Freethinking Germans who came after the revolution of 1848 were more ready to meld into the larger American society than were religious Germans of the preceding decades. Indeed, even among strong advocates of Germanness (*Deutschtum*), it was not quite clear just what constituted its essence. Was it simply a matter of familiar and cozy customs, like sitting together every day at the beer table, asked an influential promoter of *Deutschtum* in 1871. Or, he continued, did the power of German culture lie elsewhere—in such great minds as Humboldt, Uhland, Goethe,

Schiller, Kant, and Hegel?[40] But, once these great minds were brought to the center stage of consciousness, the focus of attention inevitably shifted from the local to the universal, from hearth to cosmos.

Voluntary cultural islands of the sort just described make up a significant element of American history and landscape. But most cultural islands were involuntary—products of prejudice and ignorance. Immigrants who streamed to American shores in the course of the nineteenth century disproportionately came from an impoverished rural-peasant background; and when to this handicap of poverty and cultural backwardness were added those of language, religion, and race, assimilation into middle-class American society was slow and might take several generations. This, of course, is the familiar story of immigration, the stuff of ethnic history. Each immigrant group has its own story to tell, and no doubt all the stories are different. Yet, in broad outline, there is a family resemblance. Let me recapture the lineaments of one such story, drawing on the research of Ewa Morawska. The story is that of East-Central Europeans who, in the period 1890–1940, settled in the industrial and mining town of Johnstown, Pennsylvania.[41]

Peasant immigrants, while they readily found jobs in the Johnstown area, also encountered brutally frank prejudice: they were called names (Hunkies, Dagos, Polacks), given the heaviest work, and segregated not only residentially but socially, in the sense that they were not welcome in the "better" saloons and movie theaters. A consequence of this enforced segregation was to promote ethnic communal life—the natural tendency for people of the same background to come together for encouragement, mutual help, entertainment, and relaxation. The church, with its parochial schools and parish organizations, played an important role. Church officials might disapprove of worship along lines of nationality, but there was no preventing the different immigrant groups from flocking to their own churches once they were built. The social round included weddings and funerals, church holidays, and sporting events. Gossip was rife: news of barroom fights, bankruptcies, romances, desertions, comings and goings of relatives, letters from Europe, and so on, fed and gave a certain density and warmth to communal life.[42]

Looking back, there may be a tendency to be sentimental about this ethnic communality, forgetting that it was also a limited world, created in large part under severe constraint and oppression. What did the immigrants themselves want? Well, they wanted better economic opportunities. They wanted, in this sense at least, a larger world than the one they had known in Europe. A fond image that the immigrant had of himself was to return to his village, there to be admired as an " 'Amerikanac,' a worldly traveler with endless and exaggerated stories to tell while treating others to several drinks in a nearby tavern."[43] He might be a big shot in his native village, but back in Johnstown he would once again be treated by Old Americans with condescension. And yet, there too he moved up the socioeconomic ladder, however uncertainly, after World War I. He was becoming Americanized by acquiring some of the appurtenances associated with that status: mass-produced consumer goods, a larger apartment, a house, and finally a house with a bathroom, a piano, washing and sewing machine, window curtains, and so on, in a better neighborhood.[44] Becoming Americanized meant becoming more secular. The church's hold on social life weakened as more and more activities were held outside its sponsorship. The activities themselves—song-fests, dances, educational programs, celebrations, and anniversaries—were geared to the history and culture of the Old Country.

Americanization was thus not a simple process. It did not mean a steady abandonment of the old customs in favor of the new. To the contrary, as Johnstown ethnics improved their economic condition they turned consciously to their past. They did not necessarily turn to their peasant past, which had little to offer. Rather they tried to re-create the customs and rituals of the gentry, for in doing so they could simultaneously take pride in their heritage and feel that they had moved up in the world.[45] Curiously, even while they were digging into the past, they were also broadening their horizons and showing how far they had become Americanized. They expanded their horizons by making their major celebrations transnational and by cultivating the habit of attending each other's picnics and balls.[46] They were syncretistic in their reconstruction and saw themselves as non-Anglo Europeans rather than as Slavs and Magyars. Perhaps this sort of ahistorical syncretism—this merging of distinctive groups into a larger entity—was itself a sign of modernization and Americanization. A clearer sign lay in the procedural format of ethnic organizations and social activities—in their use of ballots, in the way they conducted elections, wrote up reports of proceedings, and so on.[47]

Ethnic Consciousness, Education, and Success

Immigrants came to better themselves, and one way to do so—demonstrated over and over again—was education. Acquiring an education, though it might open the world of dominant society to newcomers, risked bringing about the weakening or loss of old customs and traditions and relaxing the tight kinship and communal bonds that enabled them to survive. Not surprisingly, the newcomers were reluctant to suffer such a loss. They wanted a better life, even to live more like "Americans" in certain material respects, but they did not clearly see education as the way. This is a familiar story. Consider again, as a case in point, the East-Central Europeans of Johnstown. Their experiences—their progress and setbacks, hopes and doubts, their tornness between allegiances to the Old Country and the New, the past and the future, an identity granted by tradition and an identity that is yet to be won—were similar to those of many other immigrant groups of peasant-rural background, and indeed they are much the same as those of the poorer immigrants in the late twentieth century.

Peasants in the Old Country considered education an adornment of the upper class, which had little practical value in their own daily struggles for survival. Important to survival were the qualities of thrift and hard work, discipline in the family such that the demands made by parents on children were like those of employer on employee, and the establishment of strong ties with kin and neighbors. These habits and ties, reinforced by prejudice in the host society, served the East-Central Europeans in Johnstown well. Improving the family's economic welfare mattered the most to them, and that meant gainful employment in a factory rather than education in a school. In 1913, a Chicago survey showed that immigrant children overwhelmingly preferred work to school even if they were not forced to work by necessity.[48] At the workplace, a young person could enjoy the camaraderie of his kin and neighbors, for factories were segregated along ethnic lines. At the public school, by contrast, he would be in an alien and unfriendly environment, where his dress, unpronounceable name, and language would be held up to scorn, where the ideals of democracy, citizenship, freedom, and individual opportunity—propagated as attainable by all—seemed at odds with his actual mistreatment and at odds also with whatever good life he knew, which was in his own community.

Parochial school was more acceptable. Religious teaching there dovetailed with social activities in the church and parish. Moral teaching largely confirmed what the children had already learned in the family—the importance of mutual help, obedience, thrift, hard work, and abiding by the social and sexual mores of the group. Academic learning in the parish school was also more sympathetic in that it stressed the student's own ethnic past—stories with which the student was already somewhat familiar—rather than the abstractions of the sciences, the constitution, civil society, and democracy. Moreover, the parish school, compared with the public school, gave less emphasis on the American value of individual achievement: progress meant communal progress—an idea that fitted well with the student's own experience.

During the interwar years, as economic conditions improved, immigrants and second-generation ethnics showed a greater interest in education. But there remained much ambivalence about its content and where to go for it—parochial or public school. On the one hand, teachers and other local leaders well versed in ethnic history and its heroes gained more respect: a conscious awareness of collective identity and pride in it increased. On the other hand, knowledge of English was a source of prestige, as also, increasingly, formal education, which came to be recognized for what it was—a powerful vehicle for social and economic betterment.[49]

The broad outline of this story of assimilation is replicated, with significant variations of detail, in many other immigrant groups of peasant-rural background. The Irish, the Scandinavians, the Italians, and the French Canadians in the nineteenth century; Hispanics (especially Mexicans) in the twentieth century; and the poorer refugees of the Vietnam War in the late twentieth century are some examples. Their stories were or are about to be success stories, in the sense that the immigrants did or are about to find a better life in the United States. But the process has been difficult and long drawn out. By contrast, immigrants with an entrepreneurial background (traders, merchants, artisans), with some education, or—more important—with a hankering for education tended to assimilate and garner the reward of dominant society faster, without necessarily losing their own cultural distinctiveness. The Japanese, Armenians, and Greeks are examples in the earlier (pre–World War II) period. Japanese immigrants, despite the fact that the law excluded them from citizenship, made heroic efforts to enter their children in high school and college. In the late nineteenth century, an Armenian parent commonly admonished his child thus: "My son, don't be ignorant like me—get an education and be a man." Note that knowledge rather than brawn or sexual prowess was associated with manhood. Greek parents, no matter how poor or lowly their social status, wanted their children to do their homework rather than housework, when these two competed for time.[50]

Strong family ties were a characteristic of the Japanese, the Armenians, and the Greeks, and strong family ties meant mutual help or reciprocity. However, unlike immigrant groups that disparaged education, those that encouraged it tended to see continuing family prosperity as dependent on the success of their young in the larger world. Parents therefore did not expect strict reciprocity; they were willing to make real sacrifices without counting on their offspring to make comparable sacrifices in quick return. Immigrants who favored education, like those who did not, held dear certain Old Country customs and traditions, and they too no doubt valued the warmth of communal feelings in the midst of their own kind, but unlike (say) the peasant immigrants of Johnstown, they were more optimistic about their ability to join mainstream society. Indeed, every good grade a child earned in school was a foretaste of success in that larger world.

The Chinese American Story

If European immigrants such as the Irish, the Poles, and the Italians encountered hostility in the United States, it is not surprising that Asian immigrants met with even greater hostility. Racism is the popular word for the attitude, but the word tends more to obfuscate than enlighten when it is loosely used as it normally is. Consider the Chinese. The gold rush of 1848 made them welcome as laborers. A governor of California in 1852 even called them "the most worthy of our newly adopted citizens."[51] But when Chinese laborers began to flood into the country from 1860 to 1880, a complete reversal of attitude took place. The newcomers were suddenly seen as aliens ("coolies") from another world, who threatened to depress not only the wages of native-born Americans but their morals. The Chinese quarters that sprang up were widely viewed as ramshackle warrens infested by gamblers, opium smokers, prostitutes, and other disreputable characters. What was the truth? In the Chinatowns of the late nineteenth and early twentieth centuries, one could find, as one could in any ongoing group, evidence of mutual help and communal sociability; one could also find commendable features distinctive to the Chinese such as industriousness, deference to elders, and respect for ancestors and the gods they had known at home. On the other hand, without doubt the Chinatowns of this period were unwholesome places in more sense than one, and not the sort of haven—dense with affection and meaning—that is justifiably associated with the more stable European ethnic neighborhoods. Early Chinatowns were largely male enclaves; the men, without the possibility of legitimate social intercourse with white women, had little choice but to resort to prostitutes. Gambling and opium smoking relieved the drabness and the claustrophobic tightness of a bounded world that owed its constriction to overwhelming prejudice on the part of white society, but also to the limitations of the migrants themselves, coming as they did from impoverished villages in the Old Country. Illiterate, ignorant, and superstitious, even in China they would have been considered backward and in need of Confucian education and enlightenment by the governing class.[52]

The Immigration Act of 1965 allowed many Chinese, as it did other Asians, to enter the United States. Whereas before World War II, the migrants came from villages in south China and were overwhelmingly male, during and after the war, and especially after 1965, they came from towns and cities in different parts of the country, including Hong Kong and Taiwan. The new migrants, compared with the old, were more sophisticated in worldly ways, better educated on the whole, and they included many women (indeed more women than men) and families. Their arrival, from the 1970s onward, caused a vast expansion and rejuvenation of the San Francisco and New York Chinatowns. Restaurants, grocery stores, movies, shops, festivals, Chinese newspapers, organizations old and new, flourished and multiplied. Space grew scarce and expensive. Adults who came with little money and few skills (including the ability to speak English) were forced to work long hours in restaurants and garment shops. Too many boys and young men, rather than resign themselves to tedious and low-paying labor as did their forebears in an earlier period, preferred the excitement and prestige of membership in gangs. Gang wars periodically flared, corroding the Chinatowns' reputation as largely crime free, a reputation they had acquired in the period from about 1940 to 1970, when they were smaller, when the influx of women and children made them more family centered than they ever were in the past, and when an important part of their business was to cater to tourists.

The surprising story in the 1970s, however, is not the gang wars in Chinatown, but rather the success of the Chinese, and of Asians generally, in American schools and universities. Precisely those institutions that are considered most impersonal, most given to dealing with abstract knowledge rather than pressing human needs, are the ones that have nurtured the Asian young. Moreover, Asian students excel in the most abstract subjects in the curriculum—music, mathematics, computer science, and the natural sciences.[53] Why these subjects? Prestige is one answer—perhaps the most important. The Chinese can see that the natural sciences are valued by society; after all, they lead to well-paid and dignified jobs. But it is the dignity that matters above all, and perhaps we see here a relic of the Confucian values that thoroughly permeate the Chinese middle class.

Two other factors enter into the choice of subjects, albeit at a less conscious level. One is the belief that mathematics and the natural sciences undergird modern affluent society. The Chinese very much want to be a part of that society. They differ from some other ethnic groups (including the East-Central Europeans of Johnstown) in wanting not only the wealth of goods that a modern society has to offer, but also the thoughts that underlie and sustain it. Finally, the Chinese and other Asians tend to see mathematics and the natural sciences as universal *human* achievements—fields of knowledge least colored by "customs and mores." Indeed, these fields of knowledge owe their success to the deliberate excision of cultural bias. Impersonal and abstract, they can for that very reason be taken up by any ethnic group without feeling that the best of its own heritage is hopelessly compromised.

Progress and Modernity

The American nation was born modern, in the Age of Reason and of optimism. Progress became an article of faith, shared widely among intellectuals and common folk alike. To the vast majority of immigrants, progress means a more affluent way of life—more possessions, to put it bluntly. Embedded in the material meaning, however, are the nonmaterial values of freedom and opportunity, and certain basic rights, including the right to pursue happiness. Progress, once anyone has taken the trouble to examine it, is readily seen to have a number of related meanings that are derived from certain dominant lines of thought among Enlightenment thinkers—a move from tyranny to democracy, from superstition and magic to science and reason, from barbarism to civility, from primitivity to culture. America's presumption has been that these kinds of progress are more likely to occur here than anywhere else, and that once they have taken root here they will spread to the rest of the world.

Such views of progress constitute a common wisdom in the United States, purveyed through a flood of school texts, Chamber of Commerce literature, industrial and technological advertisements, newspapers and popular magazines. Middle America still believes that steady improvement lies almost in the order of things. Middle America is largely white and old immigrant. But not exclusively so. The Asians who entered the country in the 1970s are neither. Yet they—those who have been exposed to Western values—are among the firmest believers in progress in all the senses mentioned earlier. Consider the Chinese. "Science and Democracy" were the slogan of the student revolutionary movement in 1919, and again in 1989, seventy years later. Progress and modernization, to the young and educated Chinese, mean science and democracy. When they cannot find them in China, they seek them in the West, above all, in the United States.

The Chinese acculturate into mainstream American life —especially academic life from high school to research university—without great stress, in part because they share with Americans certain fundamental values and prejudices. For instance, although the Chinese have never had an European-style Enlightenment, their high culture has always held rationality—an unemotional and deliberative way of looking at things—in high esteem. Magic and the supernatural, as we have noted in chapter

2, have been criticized repeatedly by Chinese scholars since at least the fifth century B.C.[54] Confucius himself chose not to consider the supernatural; and, of course, the reason why Europeans so admired the Chinese in the eighteenth century was their view of them (alas, not altogether correct) as rational.[55] The distinction between "primitive" and "cultured" or "civilized"—an increasingly important one in Europe from the sixteenth century onward—was well known to the Chinese. Indeed, the Chinese drew a sharper line between them than ever did the Europeans and, later, Americans; for, unlike romantic Westerners, the Chinese have never been admirers of peoples with simpler ways of life, such as the nomads to the north or the various non-Chinese tribes to the south, and they could not have come up with the oxymoron "noble savage."[56]

Ethnicity and Localism as Cultural-Political Ideology

The lore of American immigration goes as follows. Immigrants lead at first a harsh life. They encounter prejudice. Bigots call them names such as "Polack," "Dago," or "Chink," while the enlightened ones give them the collective label "ethnics." The term ethnic is supposedly neutral; yet, when used by Old Americans, it tends to have a condescending flavor if only because of the assumption that ethnicity is a temporal condition. As for the immigrants, their success story is that they—or, more likely, their descendants—steadily and notably improve their economic status, and in the process lose the ethnocultural characteristics (including generic ones associated with the peasantry) that set them apart. Newcomers acquire new identities: they were uneducated peasants and laborers, they become high school graduates and members of the middle class; they started as Poles (derogatorily,

Polacks), they turn into Polish Americans (ethnics), and eventually into just plain Americans. Or rather they become Americans with a certain ethnic flavor, playfully rather than aggressively retained, such as a fondness for certain foods, dressing up for national festivals, and showing a special concern for events that occur in the Old Country. By the time Americans have lived in this country for several generations, they may well have—and know that they have—multinational forebears. To a fundament of Americanness that they take for granted they are free to add extra layers of identity and heritage as fancy takes them, putting on the customs of their Polish ancestors one year and those of their Norwegian ancestors the next.

This ability to choose the sort of person one wants to be, the sort of identity one wants to have, is power—power in a free and democratic society, power that is unique to modern times. This power is political and social, but for it to be widespread and to sustain itself it has to rest on a broad base of material affluence made possible by science (in the general sense of systematically organized knowledge) and technology.

Unfortunately, many immigrant groups do not participate in this American success story, including the more recent arrivals from impoverished countries, who are still at the harshly punishing stage of their upward path, impatient to get ahead, wondering whether they will succeed, but also whether success means the loss of their own culture and strong sense of community. Such ambivalence is common among immigrants. Uprooting inevitably entails pain. Commitment to life in America has seldom been total. The degree of commitment varies, with perhaps the maximum coming from those who have suffered not only economic but political deprivation in the Old Country. All this is not new. What *is* new since the 1960s is a cultural-political ideology that asserts that people ought to be able to retain almost all the accoutrements of their original culture (language, social custom, kinship networking, and so on) and still be fully American in the sense of enjoying the nation's wealth, its full range of educational opportunities and political privileges.

This powerful ideology has its root in the sociopolitical movements that rocked the United States between the 1950s and 1970s in favor of civil rights, against the military-industrial complex and the Vietnam War, in favor of nature and the environment, against big science and its sponsoring institutions, including the large research universities. In the crudest form, revolutionary rhetoric sets up two sides. To the one side are the people and nature—heterogeneous, colorful, naturally good, creative, and steeped in life; to the other side are bloated consumers, the elite, dominant institutions, ideas, and values, a gray and geometric world. The dichotomy is also one of scale. Localism (ethnicism)—being rooted in place—is good; universalism (cosmopolitanism)—being rootless, impersonal, and artificial—is bad. Local knowledge and practice are ecologically sound; universal knowledge (science) and technology result in military hardware, or, when applied to the worthy goal of food production, they bring about irreparable damage to nature.

Praise for local lifeways combined with attack on modern society and science is not new. Also not new is wanting both the rewards of staying small, close to the familiar hearth, and the rewards (material and intellectual) of participating in a larger and richer world; for this, we have seen, was and is the ambivalent desire of many immigrant groups to America. What may well be new in the cultural politics and ideology of the late twentieth century is fervent advocacy of localism and ethnic pride joined to a demand that minorities reap the benefits of advanced technological society, and—this is the extra twist—a radical attack on that society for its hegemonic and universalizing power, not only in the political-economic and military spheres, but also in the sphere of ideas.

African and Native Americans

The dilemma of cultural contact—separatism or assimilation, ethnic integrity or melting pot, small world or large—is faced by all immigrant groups. The dilemma is exacerbated, reaching tragic proportions, in two peoples who fall outside the characterization of the United States as the land of immigrants: African Americans and Native Americans. Blacks were fully integrated into the dominant society's socioeconomic system from the beginning, but deplorably as chattel. The Civil War abolished the institution of slavery, but inequality—including the legal inequality of Jim Crow laws—persisted until the successful conclusion of the civil rights movement a hundred years later, which resulted in the removal of the more blatant racist laws and ordinances.

Nevertheless, glaring inequality remains in contemporary American society—a fact all the more galling to blacks when they see latecomers (not only Europeans but many Asians) moving more swiftly up the socioeconomic ladder. One angry response by some black leaders during the 1960s and 1970s was to urge blacks to withdraw into their own race consciousness and pride ("Black

Is Beautiful"), into their own Afro-American culture and roots in Africa, adopt African names and costumes, and certain African ceremonies and rites. In its extreme form, Africanism draws a sharp line between "fire" people (blacks) and "ice" people (whites), between those who have "soul" and those who do not, between those who live in their bodies and those who live in their disembodied heads.[57] Most black leaders, however, do not care for these provocative epithets and the degree of polarization they imply, nor do they endorse rigid separatism, which is in any case impossible in the modern global economy. They want integration into American society, its wealth and prestige, but without losing their own cultural signatures. One difficulty with this aspiration is that modern society is "soulless" to the degree that it is predisposed to become ever more secular, it is "ice" to the degree that it eschews kinship favoritism and is impersonal, and lives—increasingly so—"in the head."

Unlike black American culture, which since colonial times has meshed intimately with that of the larger society, Indian culture developed apart from Western culture and was able to confront early white settlers with notably different sets of values and achievements. Another important difference is this: Unlike blacks and almost all other immigrant groups, Indians have not sought to become "Americans," they *were* the Americans. Admittedly, this statement is marred by exaggeration, for Indians did learn on their own to appreciate certain products of Western culture. Moreover, the federal government has from the beginning urged Indians to assimilate, and a significant number of them appeared willing to comply from time to time. As for the government's policy of assimilation, it derived in part from Christian missionary zeal and in part from administrators' Enlightenment beliefs, of which two have played a major role in Indian affairs: (1) that human nature is everywhere the same and that the differences in custom and stage of culture among them are a consequence of climate and history; and (2) that human culture progresses through stages, from hunting to agriculture, commerce and industry, and sophisticated urban life. Enlightened white Americans were sincere in these beliefs. They did not doubt that Indians would be far better off fully integrated into a higher stage of social life. To their way of thinking, the Indian cultural losses were small—indeed, in some aspects even desirable (e.g., loss of certain magical and superstitious practices)—compared with all the gains that a rich civilization could provide.

The story of Native Americans in the past four hundred years, on a continent that was once their own, can only be described as at best bittersweet. Assimilation, repeatedly tried, has met with indifferent success. Returning to ancestral ways, living independently and apart from mainstream society and the federal government, is a recurrent dream, but it is likely to remain a dream. The bitterness and occasional violence of the Red Power movement of the 1960s and 1970s reveal an overwhelming sense of frustration. Much of the frustration lies in the fact that Indian leaders themselves have a hard time stating just what is best for their people. Respect for ancestral ways can be unambiguously and strongly affirmed. But there is irony even there, for Indian history and tradition—enormously varied and rich—are no longer readily accessible. To find out what really happened—who, for example, were the Mound Builders? what were Ojibwe agricultural practices like in the seventeenth century?—is difficult and perhaps impossible, or possible only if one makes use of the finest archaeological, anthropological, and linguistic research—in other words, Western science.[58]

Immigrant Sense of Insult and Injury

African Americans and Native Americans are a special case. Unlike these two groups, immigrants from other parts of the world have come to the United States voluntarily, with the intention of sharing its wealth. Yet once they are here and find life harsher than they expected, they believe that they too suffer insult and injury similar to those suffered by blacks and Indians. Following the example of Black Power and Red Power, they form power groups of their own (Chicano, Hispanic, Asian American, and so on) to protest racism and other injustices, to insist on the recognition of their own languages, customs and traditions, their own social organizations, in public institutions and places. What are the sources of this feeling of insult and injury? Prejudice is one—a fact of daily life for certain immigrant groups. Such prejudice has always been directed at newcomers; only now, in the final decades of the twentieth century, it is quite unacceptable. Economic hardship is another. In the past, new immigrants tended to take such hardship, which may last beyond the first generation, fatalistically. This is no longer quite true. Ethnic leaders, many college educated, believe in immediate empowerment, an aggressive posture that was honed during the period of civil rights and related movements. Finally—and this is perhaps the most significant new development—ethnic peoples feel insulted because their own life experiences and heritages (their hearths) have not been given proper respect in dominant society, especially in its higher educational institutions.

Demand for Cultural Justice

American universities have, in fact, always offered courses on and even established departments in non-Anglo languages and cultures. These, however, have been the recognized high European cultures (German, French, Italian, Spanish, etc.) and the great non-Western civilizations (Hindu, Islamic, Chinese, and Japanese) that have their own canons of literature, their own minutely graded standards of excellence, and their own habit of distinguishing between high art and folk art. Peasant cultures, if they are taught in an American university at all, are usually taught in an anthropology department, which traditionally treats peasant songs, dances, and artifacts as things to be explained or understood rather than as things to be admired in their own right. As for peasant-immigrant culture, or the culture of small immigrant traders and artisans, they are of little interest to scholars except as a part of immigration history and to middle-class gentry except as an early stage (still crusted over with the quaint ways and superstitions of the barely literate) that immigrants have to pass through before they are ready for proper education and modern Americanhood.

This cultural condescension, perhaps even more than economic inequality, is now deeply resented. It is bad enough to be poor, but worse to be thought poor—even rather ridiculous—in the cultural baggage and social habits that one brings to the United States. Just as blacks and Indians seek dignity in their own cultures, so do the new immigrants. Finding a sense of worth in one's heritage is not in itself new: we have seen how the East-Central Europeans have done that in parochial schools after World War I. What is new is the insistence by Hispanics, Asian Americans, and other recently arrived groups that their customs and habits, rooted in premodern realities, be judged of the same rank and dignity as the literature and art of the "high cultures" (European and non-European) traditionally studied in the universities.

Deconstructing High Culture and the Cosmos

Such insistence would have made little headway if it were not for its ability to draw righteous indignation and political support from three interwoven forces: the civil rights movement, the environmental movement, and an intellectual movement (critical theory, deconstruction) within the academy itself. The civil rights movement was a liberal-Enlightenment movement aimed at correcting racial injustice as embedded in the country's legal system. Once this was accomplished, the movement shifted attention to economic injustice, which was seen as a consequence of racism. And it eventually extended its program to include the correction of cultural injustice, which was taken to be the result of a combination of racism and class bias. The civil rights movement merged with the environmental movement in that the latter, too, could be couched in terms of the correction of an abuse—the abuse of nature by a rich and greedy society with its megatechnological machines and tentacular business corporations. The struggle in the environmental movement was and is perceived to be between something monolithic and powerful, on the one hand, and fragile nature in its infinite variety, on the other hand.

These movements—civil rights mutating into a fight for cultural equality, and environmental protection mutating into various kinds of extremism—enjoy not only the moral upperhand but even a certain intellectual cachet, thanks to a number of critical lines of thought nurtured within the universities. One line is Marxism, which attacks the excesses and presumptions of capitalist society. But far more radical is a line of thought, articulated on continental Europe in the 1960s, that criticizes (deconstructs) all megastructures, including those of thought—sweeping histories (outstandingly, those of progress—"The Rise of the West," for example), philosophical systems, large-scale works of literature and art, and scientific systems. All these megastructures are hegemonic, not only by virtue of their scale but also by virtue of a logic that, in its close-grained reasoning, suggests inevitability. These elaborately orchestrated megastructures of "high culture" put the more loosely argued miniworks of preliterate peoples, folks, peasant immigrants, ethnics, and so on, in the shade. Unjustly, in the opinion of radical critics. And one way to level the playing field is to deconstruct and fragment the larger works so that they too become or are seen as separate miniworks: we are then left with mere differences between one opinion, one work, and another, all spread out as it were on a flat plane, a colorful mosaic of sharply bounded, incommensurate units, rather than ranked judgments of ideas and works—a topography of peaks, plains, and troughs.

The intellectual temper during much of the late twentieth century is not so much critical as undermining. Western intellectual and moral edifices are undermined, as city buildings are undermined (defaced and delegitimized) by spray paint and graffiti. The drive to subvert, take down, prevent, stop, is stronger than the drive to create or build. For to build is to risk falling once more into the trap of erecting hegemonic structures. This temper or mood is dramatically different from that of the Enlightenment, a time when criticism (often severe) went alongside great hope. The critical theorists and deconstructionists of our day are particularly suspicious of eighteenth-century Enlightenment for a number of reasons. One is its belief in progress. Another is the idea of Enlightenment itself, which presupposes an earlier dark age, called sometimes "the childhood of man." The eighteenth century learned to appreciate childhood as a stage in life with its own rewards and virtues, but children were nevertheless considered emotional, dependent, subject to irrational fears, and inclined to dwell in a magical world. The founders of the United States, deeply influenced by Enlightenment thought, tended to see Native Americans, with their rain dances and shamanistic trances, as children; and very likely they saw the poorer immigrants, with their uncouth ways, as children too, to be brought up to the intellectual sobriety and responsibility of adulthood. Such a view is now abhorrent to Americans raised on the antiestablishment, antitechnology, and anti-Western passions of the 1960s and 1970s. Indeed, many are inclined to reverse the moral standing of the ages. The earlier age, when people lived in small communal groups (hearths), close to nature, propitiating it with rites and offerings, is the one to esteem and emulate. The Age of Reason, by contrast, is Western hubris.

Contradictions and Dilemmas

The cultural attitudes and ideologies of contemporary America contain a number of glaring contradictions. For example, liberal and affluent Americans, overwhelmingly white, affirm the customs and traditions of African Americans, Native Americans, and the new immigrants. They thereby demonstrate that they can transcend their own cultural bounds. Simultaneously, however, they support the view that culture is something that can be understood only by insiders, that it has boundaries that outsiders, however well intentioned and well prepared, cannot really cross. In an extreme form, this is the view that only blacks can understand the black experience, only Hispanics can understand the Hispanic experience, and so on. Both radical-liberal whites and nonwhites adopt this view because it seems to empower nonwhites. To nonwhites, it means that they and only they can really know their culture; moreover, it is a culture that they can be unreservedly proud of because it has, by definition, only peers, no superiors. With no cosmos out there to tempt them, staying home seems entirely reasonable. Confined to home by racial bias and material disadvantages, nonwhites gain the consolation that at least in matters that feed the soul (culture), they have a pearl of great price, which they may lose if they venture forth. Should this view be widely adopted and translated into reality, the United States will have multiculturalism; it will become a richly colored mosaic. But who benefits most from this type of multiculturalism? I submit, that it is well-educated whites. For they, by promoting nonwhite cultures, show their readiness to break free of their own class group. In contrast, nonwhites risk being ideologically locked into their own patch of color. By staying each within its own patch, nonwhite groups contribute to multiculturalism, but the beautiful mosaic itself is accessible only to people who can move freely beyond each particular unit, people who are, in other words, cosmopolites.[59]

Nonwhites and the nation's poorer new immigrants experience the contradictions and dilemmas deeply because they impinge on the day-to-day quality and direction of their lives. Consider one such dilemma. People embrace a cultural heritage for the warmth and distinction it provides, and for reasons of piety. However, nonwhites and new immigrants also know at a deep level and through harsh experience that their culture is the product of constraints imposed on them by a larger and more powerful society. American Indians are the exception, for, before contact with Europeans, their cultures developed under the constraint of only one dominant force—nature. All the other groups, however, have suffered humiliating, humanly imposed constraints: African Americans, outstandingly, but other groups as well, both in the Old Country, when they were peasants, and in the New, when they were baggy-trousered immigrants. Two disturbing questions arise. When the constraints (the oppression and the biases) are removed, as all must fervently wish, what remains of the culture? And an even more troubling question is, How good is a culture that has acquired its characteristic features under such severely limiting conditions?

From Color Patch to Mosaic as a Whole

Groups who have suffered in the United States wish the causes of that suffering removed so that they too can enjoy the full benefits of living here. What are these benefits? The first to be acquired is likely to be material. Thanks to mass production, many kinds of consumer goods can be purchased at modest cost. Using and enjoying mass-produced consumer goods in the home are the first step in the erosion of folk or ethnic culture. (Recall the experience of the East-Central Europeans of Johnstown.) The second general category of benefit, closely linked to the first, is to be employed in, or to own, a business that generates income. At first, this business is likely to be small—a store or restaurant that caters to neighborhood needs or to tourists in search of exotica. Such enterprises do not erode, and may indeed enhance, local culture. But as they expand, modern techniques of management and communication come into play, and traditional practices suffer as a consequence. People may eventually enter businesses that are no part of their own tradition. Examples include governmental service, work in microchip factories, running bingo parlors and casinos, as more than ten Native American tribes already do.[60] Success in these and many other modern enterprises demands a familiarity with impersonal and analytical procedures and perhaps even a whole new habit of mind that comes with prolonged exposure to formal education. These changes, needless to say, will be at the expense of long-held customs. Finally, formal education at its best leads to the critical questioning of all established positions, without somehow ending in despair.[61] And that sounds curiously like the mood and aspiration of Enlightenment thinkers!

Each step noted here is a step away from ethnic bonding and immersion in local culture. Or to put it another way, each step is a move beyond confinement within a particular color patch in the mosaic to the mosaic as a whole that is the United States. Each step is not necessarily the abandonment of a particular cultural heritage, though it does mean the loss of unreflective acceptance, or a certain innocence, that can be so assuring. As we take these steps, we come closer to recognizing that all cultures are flawed blinders as well as the source of unique illuminations, that they deserve affection rather than idolatry, that they are our first home rather than our last.

4

A COSMOPOLITE'S VIEWPOINT

China and the United States are megapolitical entities, created, respectively, over a long and a relatively short period of time. In each case, hearths have merged, without necessarily losing all trace of their original identities, into larger wholes. Often this merging has occurred by force; whence the bad reputation of cosmos. More often it has occurred through ongoing, peaceful processes of interchange and communication, voluntary imitation and assimilation. In retrospect, even this peaceful weaving and merging of hearths into larger wholes can be seen in a negative light as destructive of difference, the integrity of particular hearths, and importantly from a sociopsychological viewpoint, small ponds in which people of ordinary talent and ambition can still aspire to be big fish.

China and the United States are themselves both hearths and cosmos. They are hearths in the sense that, for all their geographic extent, they are circumscribed entities that exhibit distinctive worldviews and ways of living. On the other hand, China and the United States are also overarching cosmoses, embracing in their midst a diversity of hearths. It is possible to be in a modern high-rise building in China and believe oneself in the United States. It is not just possible but likely for someone wandering in the streets of a large American Chinatown to believe that he or she is in China. Nevertheless, while China risks looking more and more like the United States, there is no likelihood that the United States will look more and more like the China of history books and tourist guides. The reason is easily stated: the arrow of change—modernization in its many different guises—points one way, the way led by the West in the past three centuries and, in recent decades, by the United States.

China, once it became an empire, has consistently made universalist claims to rationality and humanity. Enlightened Chinese of the scholar-official class see themselves as in principle able to survey all under heaven—all within the Four Seas; and if they often also show a great affection for the microscale, the geographical and cultural uniqueness of homeplace or hearth, they do so against a background awareness of the larger world. Local custom, for example, is appreciated so long as it does not depart too far from common standards of rationality and humanity. Where it is judged too wayward, it may still be tolerated if it is geographically remote and powerless outside its own confines; otherwise it is condemned, and steps are taken to change or remove it.

Ironically, since the forced opening of China to the West, China had to entertain the disturbing idea that its universalist claim could not be upheld, that its cosmos was just another hearth, that its rationality and humanity did not go far enough, that its high culture, which tended to look down on the superstition-ridden cultures of the populace and the ethnics, itself still retained the marks of magic and other childish beliefs, that its very conception of humanity, built on the family model, was inadequate to modern longings for a more radical conception of equality and justice. Intensely upsetting to the modern Chinese was not just military defeat at the hand of the West—China had suffered major military defeats before—but rather the realization that the country's very way of thinking and its basic social arrangements were defective and needed changing.

The change was toward modernization, conceived by some Chinese intellectuals (Hu Shih outstandingly) as a human historical process rather than as the achievement of a particular people. "Science" and "democracy" are to be the twin pillars of the modern universal cosmos, under which hearths at various scales, including that of the modern nation-state, can continue to flourish: these hearths, however, will be interpolated by reflective mind and are, in that sense, "invented" and so are not the same as hearths of immemorial ways and passion.

How can China adopt "science" and "democracy," when it has suffered humiliation and injury under Western nations that claim to have invented both? How can any thinking Chinese today use these terms, as the astrophysicist Fang Lizhi has recently done, when the Chinese themselves have experimented with both, either in the guise of modern capitalist nationalism or in the guise of communism, with such mixed results? How, for that matter, can any Third World nation that has known the iron fist of the West welcome not only its scientific technology but also, at least in name, its form of government? Adoption of science by China and other Third World countries is understandable if only because its technological products yield wealth and power. But why do they embrace—or at least pay lip service to—democracy, with all that it implies in altered sociopolitical arrangements, and why do they increasingly accept Western ideas of justice and human dignity such as the presumption of innocence before trial and universal human rights?

One answer, again, is the belief, fairly widespread among the better educated, that time has direction, that it points to modernization, and that however modernization is conceived it includes a way of thinking (science), a way of governing (democracy), and, more broadly, a freer, more open form of social life. In much of the twentieth century, despite two world wars and other unspeakable horrors, people everywhere can see that Western nations have achieved for themselves a power, a degree of freedom and general well-being hitherto unknown in human history. They can probably also see that, despite the homogenizing tendencies of modernization, the Western nations have not by any means lost their unique identities, their differing senses of the collective self. With such examples before them and especially (after World War II) with the conspicuous example of the United States before them, it is easy to understand why ambitious non-Western countries should want to move in the same general direction.

Success, however, has proved elusive, or at best partial, with the outstanding exception of Japan and, more recently, such smaller Asian countries as Taiwan, Singapore, and South Korea. Lack of success, or a modest success that brings with it heavy social toll, can cause intense frustration. National and local leaders who see in attempts at modernization more social disorder than promised cornucopia might then urge a return to tradition. Surprisingly, the appeal of tradition—"the ways of our ancestors"—is not confined to marginalized nations and ethnic groups. It is a worldwide phenomenon of the late twentieth century. Powerful movements against modernization, against the overarching and overbearing modern cosmos, emerged in both the developed and developing worlds; in capitalist and former communist societies, in China and the United States. There are many reasons or causes for this turn of events, among them repugnance for communism, a ruthlessly hegemonic modern ideology, as it was experienced in the former Soviet Union and in the People's Republic of China (before, say, 1980); continuing distaste among intellectuals for capitalism—its asocial, market-driven polity, its "rational" landscape of multinational corporations; the enormous damage to the natural environment in the push toward development; the threat to variety—the earth's natural and cultural plenitudes; the decline of small neighborly communities (intimate hearths) in a cosmopolitan world of strangers; the arrogance of science—its technological and manipulative ways of thinking and doing; the illusory promises of democracy, which can seem to substitute abstract political rights for real differences in not only wealth but social-cultural status.

The leading critics of cosmos are themselves cosmopolitans. Historically, both Western and Chinese thinkers have periodically attacked society (the worldliness of the world) in favor of the simple life. What is new in the late twentieth century is the Western intellectuals' attack not only on society, but on one of their own proudest traditions—faith in reason, faith in the possibility of approximating truth through the removal of personal and cultural bias. The more extreme postmodernist intellectuals argue, instead, that there can exist only relative truths, personal and contextual truths, each (as it were) an island or hearth, with its own distinctive qualities and characteristics that are no better or worse than those of other hearths.

One can well understand, at least in retrospect, the popularity of this view. It touches base with disillusioned cosmopolitans who can see the large picture and dread what they see—cultural uniformity and environmental havoc, consequences, ultimately, of the tyranny of reason. But intellectuals can have little influence on society at large unless their views tap into ordinary people's experiences and beliefs. And in this instance they have done so. They are able to articulate the frustration and resentment of all the people who, in both developed and developing countries, have not achieved a hoped-for material standard of living, and who, even when they have done so, still do not feel that they are fully contributing citizens of the modern cosmos.

We see, worldwide, a resurgence of pride in local culture. This movement is powerful enough to promise the reestablishment (in some fashion) of the earth's former cultural diversity, to slow down the pace or even alter the character of the march toward global "sameness" that almost all the modern technologies of manufacturing, marketing, and communication promote. Cultural diversity—a richly patterned world—is indisputably desirable; moreover, if the movement toward it succeeds in multiplying values, including a significant number that cannot be satisfied by modern market economies, it will also have a positive effect, however indirect, on biodiversity and the environment. As we have noted earlier, the concept "diversity"—the confluence of many hearths in one great place—is itself fully compatible with and is indeed a major defining characteristic of cosmos. Cosmopolites and cosmopolitans welcome pluralism, fearing it only when it threatens to become anarchic and destroy the very idea of cosmos—the notion that human beings have important common experiences, that in view of these experiences and in view, further, of the powers of the imagination, it is entirely possible for one person to stand in the shoes of another, for one people to understand and appreciate the worldview of others.

Pride in one's culture can be a force for good or evil. Much depends on the nature of this pride, whether the emotion is tempered by self-criticism and a knowledge of the larger world, or is ignorant and fanatical. A disturbing turn in our late twentieth century is the dramatic efflorescence of fanatical pride, a deliberate narrowing of life to one's own culture and corner of the world. Such turns have occurred in the past. What makes the turn ("culturalism," to give it a name) distinctive in our time is its patronage by intellectuals who, though they may have grown disenchanted with the modern world, retain one of its most idealistic sentiments, namely, radical egalitarianism.

Radical egalitarianism demands an attitude of deep suspicion toward not only modern civilization but toward all civilizations on account of the one feature they have in common: each is in its own way a vast edifice of knowledge. In a small community, the potential for equality of knowledge, the ultimate basis of sociocultural equality, is real: what the headman knows in lore and practical skill is what everyone can know. In a complex civilization, on the other hand, even when a large measure of juridical-political equality exists, as in a modern democracy, the distribution of knowledge remains highly uneven. There is no shortcut to learning, which is not only the ticket to respected jobs and professions but also to civilization's great works of literature, art, and science, many of which do not begin to yield their full power without sustained study. Education for citizenship in the cosmos has always been a prolonged and difficult process. It has never seemed more so than in modern times, for at least two reasons: ready availability (thanks to increasingly efficient print and electronic media) of the world's accumulated wisdom, which looms over the learner like an accusation, and the rapid growth of new knowledge. Even among young people in affluent Western countries, not only the opportunity but the desire for sustained education is limited. Without such education a sense of cultural marginality and social inferiority is hard to avoid, unless one takes the draconian step of denying the merit of the modern cosmos, especially its towering scientific edifice, and embrace with vehemence "timeless" traditions and beliefs.

In the absence of an alluring great world "out there," one's own patch of earth, one's own intimate and direct experiences, become all that is necessary to one's fulfillment as a human being. This posture, for all its extremity, easily catches fire; and if the fire had been banked beneath a layer of cosmopolitanism it readily reignites under the prodding of local leaders who, for both high-minded (though often misguided) and low-minded reasons, seek to exploit their people's feelings of resentment and insecurity. Such feelings are more deeply rooted in our psyche and more widespread than we, even the sophisticated, like to admit. Culturalism is natural to us, as true multiculturalism is not. Again, bonding based on propinquity and kinship is natural to us. By contrast, kindness to strangers who may not reciprocate and civility in impersonal transactions are a watermark achievement of civilization.

I should now like to attempt three things, all of which seek to restore the cosmos and the cosmopolite's viewpoint to a position of greater respectability. First, I shall draw attention to certain moral-intellectual weaknesses in "culture and community" (hearths), suggesting that they, for all their essentiality to social cohesion and individual survival, deserve two rather than three cheers. Second, I shall highlight certain merits of "civilization and society" (cosmos), suggesting that their current location in the doghouse is a bias, an inordinate reaction against the pride and excesses of intellect, that threatens to deprive us of all inspiration, of the very possibility of moving from "home" to "world." Third, I shall argue in favor of hearths, not as founts of nostalgia, however sweet and consoling, or as political bases in the struggle for advantage and power, however necessary in establishing social justice, but as a fundamental habitus, along with cosmos, for beings like us—beings that possess both body and mind.

Culture

Culture sets limits, and a particular culture sets a particular set of limits. Limits to what? Limits to experience—to the sensations and impressions that can disorient and disable even when, in isolation or in small packages, they are benign and welcome. Two metaphors—house and spectacles—usefully underline certain basic functions of culture. Culture is a house or haven. Inside the house, people are protected by walls, the roof, and other boundaries from sensations that they do not want. At the same time, enclosed spaces within the house have a way of heightening sensations that people do want, such as warmth from a fire or in the more intimate human contacts, fragrance from cooked food or from a flowering tree in the gently stirred air of a courtyard. Cultures differ in the rigidity and sharpness of their boundaries. The house again serves as an illuminating metaphor. The courtyard house, a feature of civilizations since the earliest times, confronts the external world with high windowless walls. Many traditional houses and residential compounds sharply distinguish between interior and exterior space, thereby emphasizing their function as haven. By contrast, a modern house with large picture windows, sliding glass doors, and patios that extend to unfenced lawns, almost constantly reminds its occupants of the existence of a larger world. Some cultures, it is true, do not have permanently walled-in spaces or houses, but they do have, as of course all human groups do, moral codes, or moral edifices, to stay with our architectural metaphor. Moral codes differ in rigidity; moral edifices differ in size, in the number of partitions, and in their degree of openness. Nevertheless, despite such variations and despite the provisioning of a security that can foster a desire for exploration, their fundamental reason for being is to define and delimit, to protect and nurture by means of confinement. Culture's ambivalence is that of walls and houses: walls that attempt to keep all dangers out lock people in, and houses that are effective shelters risk becoming prisons.

Culture as house emphasizes its confining and protective roles. Culture as spectacles emphasizes its focusing and sharpening powers. We need culture as astigmatic people need corrective lenses. Without them, people with poor eyesight find themselves in a fuzzy and disorienting world, in which they cannot operate with any confidence. Unfortunately, all spectacles are tinted—if I may embroider my figure of speech. Each human group has its own spectacles with their own characteristic tint. Different groups recognize the same features in the landscape, but cannot agree on their color. Some see the landscape as blue, others as green or red. And since color is emotion laden, people are heatedly convinced that others are seeing incorrectly, arbitrarily, or even perversely. How can a warm red landscape be described as blue? One can try on spectacles of a bluish tint, but this means removing those one has always had, which immediately produces sensations of dizziness and disorientation. Why proceed further? Most people don't: the tinted world they know seems not so much the best as the only real one. Suppose one group claims that it has managed to remove all tint from its spectacles, that they have become totally transparent, that they enable people to see the world for the first time as it really is. Won't the other groups deny the claim as arrogant and false, and won't they, once they discover that the claim is plausible, proceed to denounce the picture of the world thus revealed as soulless and lacking emotional appeal?

Culture is most commonly understood as custom, that is to say, a habitual practice, the usual way of acting in a given circumstance. Dictionaries, however, provide another, more sophisticated definition of custom, namely, a collective convention. "Why do you act this way?" the ethnographer asks. Answer from native informant: "Because we have always done so, because that's the way of our ancestors, because it is the right way." Culture or custom is so ingrained in our being, in how we act in the small and large challenges of life, that most of us will unthinkingly respond in a similar manner. But, having been exposed to the cosmos, we also accept, with our mind rather than viscerally, the idea that custom is a collective convention, that it can be otherwise than what it is. Consider an example from the Western world. After Schubert's death, his brother cut some of his musical scores into small pieces, of a few bars each, and gave them to the composer's favorite pupils. As a sign of piety, this act can seem rather bizarre. Yet, is it any less bizarre and arbitrary than if the custom had been different, if the brother had kept the scores in a deep vault, accessible to no one, or if he had burned them?[1]

Piety is an emotion as well as a set of gestures. Separating the two presents almost insuperable difficulties both to the pious individual and to the community that observes and judges him. To the individual, the expression that piety takes is not merely an outward form, for it can focus and enhance his feeling. As for community, it has no way of knowing whether a person is pious other than by attending to what he does. Cutting Schubert's scores into little pieces comes to *be* piety for Schubert's brother and for the community to which he belongs. Burning the scores would be an outrage. In some other community and culture, it may well be that applying the scissors to a beloved person's lifework is the unnatural act. What this example makes clear is the lack of any necessary relation between a particular cultural practice and the feeling it is supposed to express. *Some* outward expression is not only natural but necessary if the feeling is to be sustained and channeled: it just does not have to be a particular one. Yet people can find one another repellent over differences in custom. And they will continue to do so unless they are able to see that their custom, for all its air of ultrahuman sanction and primordiality, is a collective convention.

Community

Community, like culture or hearth, is a good warm word that evokes nostalgia among many cosmopolitans. Broadly understood as any network of mutual support and sympathy, community flourishes now as it has done in the past; indeed, there may be more types of cooperative networks today than there ever were in the past. What appears to be missing and is missed is a particular type of traditional community, captured by the words "village" and "neighborhood," in which everyone has his or her place, in which hardly anyone is overlooked, uncared for, and alone. This ideal community of nostalgia probably never existed. Even if something like it did exist, cosmopolites and cosmopolitans will feel uncomfortable in it for a number of reasons, including community's historical root in toil and struggle, in scarcity; its suspicion of the larger world, its psychological need to see outsiders and strangers in a hostile or dismissive light; its narrow and frankly egocentric conception of mutual help; its social immobility (it is one thing to have a place but quite another to know one's place or to be put in one's place); its indifference to the uniqueness of the individual, to individual destiny as distinct from communal well-being. Let me elaborate.[2]

The true community, Martin Buber writes, is a community of tribulation, toil, and work.[3] Work, yes, we may say: work, including mental work, is essential to any kind of community. But tribulation and toil? Here Buber seems to have in mind a world of scarcity, in which people gain cohesion in their common fight against an external enemy. Historically, the external enemy to fend off and exploit is nature. Hence the village is the archetypal community. Villagers have to cooperate to wrest a living from nature and to protect themselves against its ravages. They may dislike one another, but the dislike is repressed by the exigencies of teamwork. In a city, there is less toil, at least among the well-to-do, but tribulation remains, the external enemy remains, and with it the development of intensely bonded communities. The external enemy in the city is not so much nature as a rival human group: one thinks of Shakespeare's Verona and of how the feud there between such great families as the Montagues and the Capulets has generated a strong sense of communal solidarity. Cities and city-states, historically, have been able to strengthen group pride through rivalry and war. Even the large and unwieldy nation-state, under military threat from a powerful enemy, becomes a warmly cohesive whole. People who confess to feeling a certain nostalgia for past wars miss the simplified life of ardor and social cohesion.

Communal bonding requires an external other. But this other, though a necessary requirement, does not explain how relationships within the community are established and maintained. One device is the regular exchange of goods and services. Not only a deep awareness of interdependence but affection can emerge as a consequence. However, since exchange within a premodern community is dictated by stringent necessity, there is also inevitably a large element of calculation; indeed, the idea of an outright gift seldom occurs. The village or tribal chieftain who dispenses material largesse and patronage expects immediate compensation in deference and (sooner rather than later) in services if not goods. As M. I. Finley puts it, "The word 'gift' is not to be misconstrued. It may be stated as a flat rule of both primitive and archaic society that no one ever gave anything, whether goods or services or honors, without proper recompense . . . to himself or to his kin. The act of giving was, therefore, in an essential sense always the first half of a reciprocal action, the other half of which was counter-gift."[4]

Reciprocity is at the heart of moral behavior and communal life. Yet there is this calculation and manipulation that, in a traditional village, extend beyond human beings to the deities and spirits of nature, who are considered members of the community in a larger sense. In both the ancient Greco-Roman world and in premodern China, one can find numerous examples of how nature deities were propitiated, coaxed, and even threatened so as to yield the expected material blessings. It seemed unconscionable to people that the gods and goddesses did not reciprocate when given offerings. A frequent formula of Roman prayers was *do ut des* (I give so that you will give). As for Chinese peasants, they might threaten a nonreciprocating or laggardly deity with the higher authority of the emperor, or do something drastic to him themselves.[5] We have seen in chapter 2 how an uncooperative god could be dealt with: his image was left for hours in the burning sun so that he would be stirred by his personal discomfort to do something about the drought he was being asked to alleviate.

Reciprocity produces a bond or bonding. These are good words, yet they are uncomfortably close to bondage. Intimate human ties can be deeply ambivalent, with the good feelings yoked to their opposites. The meaning of the preposition "with" is, in this respect, suggestive: it is both "together" and "against." The clinch of love is, in its outward manifestation, much like the clinch of combat, and if we go along with the thesis of David Gilmore, combat itself is a way of cementing communal ties.[6] Hostility, in other words, is a kind of mutuality. Language captures the paradox in that the word "hostile" has the same root as "hospitable." The host who comes to you with open arms is showing his—to use Frederic Cassidy's neologism—"hospitility."[7]

Although hostility, within limits, can actually form bonds, it easily becomes violent and disruptive. Consider the family, which is the archetype of communal warmth. In the family, members help and care for one another as a matter of course. But in a constricted world of stark needs and of human ties that are unbreakable, feelings of frustration and anger can reach the highest intensity. Peter Laslett, speaking of the premodern family, says that "the worst tyrants among human beings, the murderers and villains, are jealous husbands and resentful wives, possessive parents and deprived children . . . Men, women and children have to be very close together for a very long time to generate the emotional power which can give rise to a tragedy of Sophocles, or Shakespeare, or Racine."[8] Many close-knit groups project an outward air of calm and mutual solicitousness. Indeed, the physical proximity of dwellings in certain villages and urban neighborhoods suggests closeness and human warmth: people stand by or lean on one another as houses do. Nevertheless, behind the walls we should not be surprised to find tragicomedies of betrayal, or lives stunted or cut short in a world of febrile intimacy rarely relieved by the light of impersonal understanding.

Civilization: Culture as Technology

Culture as custom—how people behave and what they make in the domestic sphere—encourages an impression of equality and difference throughout the world; thus English culture with its boiled cabbage and Morris dancing is on a par with, yet amusingly different from, Eskimo culture with its blubber meals and football games played with a walrus skull. Culture, however, may also be defined as the means by which a people gain control over their environment. The focus then is on technique and technology as sources of power. Nowhere is this activist (aggressive) meaning of culture more evident than in the history of the West, beginning with the ancient Greeks. A famous choral ode in Sophocles' play *Antigone* is a paean to technique. It describes how the arts and the sciences have brought human beings, step by step, from helplessness to a mastery of nature and to their crowning achievement, which is the sociopolitical state. *Techne*, the ode seems to say, makes it possible for people to make themselves immune to luck—to "what just happens to a man" as opposed "to what he does or makes."[9]

Technique, in the original Greek meaning, is focused knowing. Know the nature of things and then bring what is inherent in them into the open. Language is a technique of naming and addressing. Objects, named and addressed, come into their own as though freshly created. Rituals are a technique. A palpable world can be called into existence by a combination of evocative words and ritual gestures. Technique has always implied power: it is the method that generates power, which can be more or less intrusive. To dance well, one applies technique to the body, making it do what one wants. Cutting down trees efficiently with an ax demands technique. Organizing men so that they as a team can assault a forest, build a city, dig irrigation canals, and otherwise transform nature is technique. Technique turns into technology as personal and social (organizational) skills shift to engineering knowledge and its products.

Cultures differ markedly in the techniques and technologies at their disposal. Those with more have applied them to create extensive artificial worlds that are sometimes called "civilizations."

An artificial world or civilization aspires to be cosmos—that is, substitute not only the regularity but also the magnificence of heaven for the drab uncertainties of life on earth. Yearning for cosmos is rooted in a high sense of human dignity—in the belief that human beings cannot just be creatures of the day, constrained by forces beyond their comprehension or control, and relieved by visceral pleasures that differ little from those of other animals. True, for millennia, only a small elite could aspire to be gods, but once that possibility lay open to more people lower down the social scale—thanks in part to technical inventions that have shifted the balances of power—they too found its allure irresistible.

Civilization is practically synonymous with city; in particular, the great city of monumental buildings and diversified populace that stands for the world, or cosmos. The city is the single most powerful image of the cosmos, and as such it lies at the opposite pole of terrestrial nature in its two aspects of primordial chaos and raw, exigent organic life. Technique and technology transform nature into artifact and artifice. Thousands of years ago, society already knew how to organize human beings into large, finely integrated work teams—the world's first "megamachines" (Lewis Mumford)—that possessed the power to level hills and divert streams, and so produced the sort of even surface on which geometric cities could be built.[10] History textbooks begin their stories of civilization in Mesopotamia, the Indus Valley, the Huang Ho basin, and Mesoamerica, with such earth-transforming ventures. If a village may be considered a giant house for human beings, sheltering them from the elements, then the city may be considered a giant palace that does much more than just protect its inhabitants from the elements: it provides them with a handsome stage for conducting social and cultural affairs. Significantly, in extratropical cities these reach a peak in the winter half of the year, when life in the countryside slows down or becomes dormant. We may well see the city and its institutions, from ancient to modern times, as a technique for defying winter, generating their own sort of exuberance and plenitude as nature's decline.

Technology and the Overcoming of Darkness

If winter cold was a challenge to human ingenuity, the challenge of darkness was even greater and far more difficult to overcome. The need and desire to overcome it have always been there, for human beings are primarily visual animals, with eyes that in daylight see the world as a palette of colors, sharply delineated, an invitation to life. Night, by contrast, is a dark, disabling presence, silence, loss of consciousness, or a consciousness haunted by dreams and nightmares. To be fully human is to live in the light. Our earliest cave-dwelling ancestors hovered around a fire, which gave not only warmth but light—the pool of light that enabled them to see and converse intimately with one another, and so cement society.[11]

Whereas human labor teams, aided by certain simple mechanical devices, made it possible for the Egyptians to build giant pyramids by the middle of the third millennium B.C., their technologies of illumination (candles and open-flame oil lamps) could provide them with only dim flickering light. Astonishingly, these primitive technologies remained little changed until the approach of the nineteenth century. Paris, which eventually earned the title "City of Lights," could hardly have entertained such ambition before 1800. In the seventeenth century, despite the 6,500 lanterns ordered by the chief of police, the city, with the exception of a few streets, was inky black.[12] Even in the mid-nineteenth century, a French country doctor on call at night to attend his patient blessed the full moon. Around 1800, people all over the world, whether they were affluent or poor, citizens of a metropolis or villagers, shared the common experience of darkness after sunset. No culture then was decisively superior to another in this crucial matter of illumination: black night imposed a democracy of voicelessness on all.

This equality before a fact of nature changed when one people in one part of the world invented first gas, and then electric, lighting. With the wide application of gaslighting, we can speak for the first time of the conquest of darkness on any scale. With the wide use of electric lighting in the twentieth century, we can truly say that, in some great metropolises, the day has swallowed night, and that human beings, by exercising their technical ingenuity, have learned how to curtail a fundamental rhythm of nature. In time, the extent and quality of a city's night life were accepted as a critical measure of its urbanity and sophistication. In any city worthy of the name, twilight presaged not withdrawal but a new burst of activity on its well-lit boulevards. The city, with electric illumination, acquired a new sense of glamour, the root meaning of which is magic. By merely flicking on switches, a modern city, drab perhaps during daytime, is transformed into a glittering world at night. People, too, discard their workaday personalities for fancier masks. In theaters and cinemas, concert halls and nightclubs, the irritating incompletion and messiness of real life are left behind for the sonorities of music, the clarities and resolved passions of stage and screen. Night life is unnatural. As daylight fades, so should human consciousness. In flourishing cities, however, it reaches a new height.[13]

Overcoming darkness has figurative as well as literal meanings. Light signifies spiritual illumination in the major world religions, outstandingly Buddhism and Christianity. In the West, it also signifies reason, as the expression—the Enlightenment—makes clear. Eighteenth-century European thinkers, in their pride and confidence, believed that the light of reason would sooner or later dispel ignorance and superstition. The nineteenth century and a little beyond (ca. 1830-1910) saw another surge of European confidence. Gas and electricity that so efficiently and dependably illuminated European and American cities in that period presented a dramatic token, among other accomplishments in engineering and technology, of the power of reason to free people from bondage to nature and to belief in magic that multiplied in ignorant fear.

An unfortunate consequence of success of this magnitude in one part of the world was that it made the rest seem darker and more backward by comparison. The West became insufferably arrogant. Although the most egregious display of that arrogance was in the political-imperial arena, the attitude, that air of superiority, was fully evident in other areas of life as well; and its ultimate source lay in the pride of mind. After World War II, as empires crumbled and as technology itself was beginning to be considered too intrusive and imperial, bestowing at best mixed blessings, the use of intellect in a certain way and reason itself came under attack. At first, the disgruntlement was restricted to a small minority of humanist intellectuals; later, especially in the waning decades of the twentieth century, it spread among substantial numbers of young people (often with some form of liberal arts education) throughout the world.

Nevertheless, light as a metaphor for reason and spirituality remains potent. It is, after all, not confined to one particular people, culture, or time: it may be a way of thinking rooted in common human experience. At a practical level, even harsh critics of Western technology are unwilling to go back to candlelight, if only because poor lighting diminishes the possibilities of human exchange and communication, and so, in effect, political power. At a figurative level, we still speak readily of a "bright mind" or "bright idea," and of education as bringing light to young minds. Illumination is a good word wherever it is used. Attacking human reason, unless it is in the name of divine reason, which wears an even brighter halo, is a sure path to chaos and the night. But a complicating factor intrudes. Chaos, its liberating potential notwithstanding, remains essentially undesirable; by contrast, darkness or night, as a time of regenerative rest, can have the strongest appeal, and perhaps never more so than now, for it is also a respite from an excess of consciousness that is a signal affliction of our time.

Individuals and the Cosmos

The city embodies human aspiration, confidence, and power. It does so as architecture, in its individual monumental buildings and in its planned totality (the cosmos). It does so, moreover, as social setting. In the city, people build up an image of human possibility as they observe, and learn to participate in, an extraordinary range of activities undertaken, peacefully, by individuals and groups who are strangers to one another. So, there is life—exciting life—beyond the neighborhood; and there is cooperation, too, on a scale beyond that conceivable in a village. With greater security both from nature and from strangers, city people feel less need for that tightness of communal bonding typical of rural life; they are freer to move about geographically and socially, freer to be themselves, freer to think—indeed, *forced* to think, if only because they are constantly encountering other groups that hold different values and viewpoints.

Individualism varies among cultures, being more prominent among hunters and nomads than among sedentary peasant-farmers, more prominent in modern than in premodern societies. Contrary to popular belief, individualism is not a unique characteristic of the West. Indeed, one might argue that Hindu civilization, by trying to convince its religious adepts to value their own personal liberation above all else, promotes individualism of an extreme self-regarding kind. Communal life can hardly flourish if, in accordance with Upanishad teaching, the self is dearer not only than wealth but than one's kinfolk, even dearer than a son. Why dearer? The answer is: "He who reverences the self alone as dear is not perishable."[14] Individualism, in recent decades, has taken on the almost wholly negative meaning of selfishness. But that is not its sole or even principal meaning. Individualism can and does also mean, benignly, a person's awareness of his or her own distinctive qualities, the desire to use them for his or her own delight, benefit, even salvation, as well as for the well-being of the group to which he or she belongs; an awareness of the wealth of human relationships that can be entered into freely, of the depth of the self and the wideness of the external world, and the possibility of joining the two. Individualism is a demonstration and an effect of thought: its most characteristic mark is a certain (psychological) distancing from both the habits and the passions of the group.

To illustrate these positive meanings and, at the same time, reinforce the idea that individualism, though more evident in one culture than another, more prevalent in modern than premodern times, is by no means restricted to either any particular culture or any particular historical period, let us consider merchants, Buddhist monks, and Greek thinkers.

Merchants in a World of Commerce

A city that is not cosmic in an architectural-ritual sense may yet be cosmopolitan in that it is where a heterogeneous population assembles. People may come from afar to benefit from the opportunities and excitement of a great city. Prominent among such people are traders and merchants, for whom place is location with economic advantages. In contrast to farmers, merchants worship no local gods. They recognize the genius of place, for it is their business to know its characteristic products. It is also their business, however, to uproot and disperse them. Their inclination toward the abstract is promoted by the fact that, although they recognize the qualities of goods and are constantly persuading their customers to do the same, they see goods ultimately as figures in the ledger.

Merchants form guilds and associations, which are their own forms of community. These may or may not be located in their native towns. Membership in such guilds and associations favors kinsmen and former neighbors, but cannot be confined to them. A brotherhood of common economic interests rather than of blood is essential. To be successful, traders and merchants must be individualists with enough imagination to break out of the mold, move and travel, take calculated risks, and not only tolerate but know strangers—their habits and tastes, what they want or can be persuaded to want. An itinerant peddler, commanding the market of a couple of streets, may have no higher ambition. Yet it is the nature of commerce to be open-ended. An ambitious peddler may end up a merchant prince with the world as his market. A peddler is a cosmopolite, not only because he is at ease in the midst of strangers, but also because, potentially, he can operate on an extraregional and even global scale.

Buddhist Individualism and Universalism

Merchants and monks live in different worlds. Commerce and religion designate separate, incompatible spheres of activity. Yet certain overlaps are evident, historically and in value orientation. Universal religions coexist, if not with universal empires, then with burgeoning kingdoms and cities—with the expansion of trade and a dramatic broadening of intellectual horizon. All these categories—merchants and monks, commerce and empire, universal religion—evoke space and spaciousness as distinct from place and hearth, a compact between self and some large, abstract whole that tends to make light of all the concrete, intermediate scales of bonding. Consider Buddhism. Buddha (the Enlightened one, as he came to be known) was born when kingdoms and cities were displacing oligarchic chiefdoms, small towns and villages, on the middle Gangetic plain. People sought a better life and were no longer content to remain fatalistically in place. As more and more of them moved about from city to city, customs began to loosen their grip and social life became more fluid. Even a custom as ancient and strong as caste was shaken. A rich merchant, for example, might have an impoverished Brahmin as his servant. The merchants, themselves not designated separately in the original caste system, had to be accommodated as their number and influence increased. Still newer occupations emerged from 500 B.C. onward, such as salaried officials and paid soldiers, which further strained a social system based on an ancient agricultural-pastoral way of life.

Cities on the middle Gangetic plain acquired a cosmopolitan flavor. Vendors and merchants of different background assembled in one place, where they were obliged to exercise mutual tolerance if not mutual appreciation; likewise, itinerant teachers and ascetic seekers after truth. The bolder of these were confident enough of their views to defend them against rival claims in the city's public halls. For such debates to be fruitful, those who participated in them had to learn an abstract way of thinking and of speaking, accept general criteria of truth, recognize means of differentiating valid reasoning from mere assertion. Buddha himself entered such debates. He excelled in combining high abstraction with concrete detail drawn from ordinary life. He expounded universal truths concerning human nature and the laws of moral causation; on the other hand, he was also able to offer practical steps toward liberation that sounded convincing to their listeners because they drew on profound psychological insights.[15]

Although human beings shared a common nature, no two individuals lived through the same stream of experience. Liberation required each person to be fully awake to his or her unique stream of mental states, intentions, and actions, for all of them would have inevitable moral consequences. It was this emphasis on the individual, which Buddha shared with other teachers of his time, that enabled him to wave aside ancient social distinctions: a Brahmin stood as much in need of enlightenment as the humblest artisan.[16] But what was to follow from such individual salvation? Legend has it that Buddha, after his own success and after mulling over his discoveries, wondered whether there was any point in announcing them to a world sunk in ignorance and delusion. A god convinced him that there was, that he and his followers should remain incarnate and show compassion for suffering creatures by bringing light into their deluded lives. Service to others did not, however, alter the order of priority, which, logically, had to remain the same. First, that bundle of psychic energy called "self" must be liberated; then and only then could help be extended to other creatures.

Among Buddha's earliest converts were fellow seekers after truth and members of the mobile merchant class. An affinity existed between them based on rootlessness and a shared attitude of searching—even though what they originally searched for could not be further apart. Buddha's followers, who were required to be celibate mendicants (monks), enjoyed membership in small, loosely structured communities, each with its own rules of procedure, its own constitution. The monks were not enclosed in these communities; their ideal was not that of *stabilitas loci*. Indeed, monks were duty bound to travel and spread their message of liberation far and wide, and since they lacked their own means of sustenance they had to establish quickly a relationship of mutual dependence with the laypeople, exchanging spiritual food for material nurture. It is another link between monks and merchants that the roads along which Buddhism diffused were built in the first place to facilitate trade.[17]

Monks and merchants were cosmopolitans, basically indifferent to where they lived. But monks were also cosmopolites, habitants of a vast universe. A conception of space and time on a scale unmatched until the discoveries of modern astronomy was an outstanding trait of Hindu and Buddhist thought. To religious Hindus and Buddhists wedged in between, on the one side, the arduous path of individual enlightenment and, on the other side, the overmastering immensity of the cosmos, human communities and institutions, human sociopolitical aspirations, could seem unimportant and transient.[18]

Greek Thinkers and Their Cosmos

Buddha lived in a time of rising Indian civilization. Ancient Greek thinkers who still command our admiration today lived in a time of rising Western civilization. Busy trade cities provided sympathetic settings for the evolution of thought. Miletus could claim Thales and Anaximander as active citizens: both were fully engaged in its political and economic affairs. Samos, a powerful and progressive city-state famed for its artists and boldly inventive engineers, could claim Pythagoras. Heraclitus was born and lived out his life in the prosperous commercial city-state of Ephesus.

Thinkers of the Greek Enlightenment easily dismissed the divine couplings and mythological dramas of their own tradition. They considered the cosmos admirable in itself; and in this attitude they moved, in cool impersonality, even beyond the Buddhists, for whom the cosmos served primarily as a vast stage in the unfolding of human, superhuman, and nonhuman destinies. In distinction to other peoples, the Greeks also sought to understand, as though under some kind of metaphysical compulsion or yearning, the fundamental nature of things. Could the ultimate principle for such understanding be water? Thales thought so. Anaximander, who rejected water as fundamental, rejected the other elements as well in favor of some indeterminate entity that lay "behind" them. Pythagoras, inspired by his discovery of musical scale, saw the whole world (which he was the first to call "cosmos") as harmonious. Pythagoras and his followers carried thought further into the abstract realm when they considered *form* rather than *substance* to be crucial to the constitution of things. And since mathematics was singularly efficient and precise in describing form, it came to be regarded as the key to true knowledge.

Greek thinkers gave rise to the image of the lofty-minded man who contemplated the stars as he walked, and so fell into a hole in the ground, to the amusement of onlookers. Anaxagoras was an early exemplar of this type of otherworldliness. He gave away his property and in doing so, he forfeited citizenship, which depended on having a permanent hearth. When he was asked, "Have you no care for your country?" he replied, pointing to the sky, "I have great care for my country." The anecdote, according to J. V. Luce, established him as the first explicit cosmopolite, someone who owed "allegiance to scientific truth rather than to Athens or Clazomenae." Another Greek who exalted truth above all worldly power and wealth was Democritus. To him was attributed the saying, "I would rather discover one causal explanation than possess the kingdom of Persia."[19]

Early thinkers of the Ionian school directed their attention primarily to the physical universe. By the middle of the fifth century B.C., philosophers, mostly Athenians, began to show a greater interest in human nature and the world of human affairs. The rift that the Ionians opened up between their progressive science and ordinary people's religious beliefs continued and grew possibly larger when the Athenians turned their critical intellect on human beings. Prominent among the early humanists were itinerant teachers called Sophists, who earned a livelihood teaching their pupils the techniques of effective speaking, these techniques having grown more important to success as public life became more open and democratic. An emphasis on techniques of success might invite conformism, but such was not the case, perhaps because the early Sophists laid stress on the need to exercise personal judgment and were, moreover, themselves outstanding individualists.[20] The best of the Sophists were public-minded men, concerned to show their pupils the path to the common good. To achieve the common good, a thoughtful citizen's point of departure must remain the careful weighing of a question addressed to the self. Thus Socrates, considered a Sophist by his contemporaries, sought to serve Athens by persuading its young aristocrats to ask seriously, "How should a man lead his life?" Thinking hard and critically about self and society, taking none of the currently held values for granted, was urged by Socrates on his followers at every turn. From community's standpoint, such critical thinking could be subversive in the extreme. Rather than promote a tolerance for different viewpoints and customs, it could lead to unrestrained cynicism. Socrates himself was able to combine radical doubt with deep respect for legitimate institutions. He even showed a fond regard for custom: his last words were, "Crito, we owe a cock to Asclepius [god of healing]."[21] But even the best of possible worlds cannot hope to have many Socrates.

Early Greek philosophers postulated, on the one hand, the thinking individual and, on the other, the cosmos. Each thinker could claim to be a "citizen of the universe," as Anaxagoras did. Later Greek philosophers, by contrast, emphasized a different dyad—the individual and the public good. But, as in the earlier period, individual cultivation remained all important. The sort of things that normally held communities together—reputation, honor, money—were to be set aside in favor of acquiring knowledge of good and evil and elevating one's own soul. Perfecting the self was central to Socrates, as it was to Plato, Platonists, Stoics, Christian and non-Christian thinkers, right down to our contemporary, Ludwig Wittgenstein, who liked to say to his friends, "Just improve yourself. That is all you can do to improve the world."[22]

To Buddhist and Greek thinkers alike, individual enlightenment enjoyed priority. As Plato's famous cave myth teaches, one must first come out of the cave and see reality in the light of the sun before one can return to help others still living in and enthralled by a world of flickering shadows. Now comes the crucial question that has endlessly stirred debate among Western political and social thinkers. When the philosopher returns to the cave, what exactly is he to do? Improve the cave's lighting in small increments or persuade others in the cave to abandon their habitual abode altogether?

Greek Enlightenment, like that of eighteenth-century Europe, was infused by an optimism based on faith in the fundamental rationality and capacity for good of human beings. Such faith made radical change seem justifiable and possible. Historically, however, utopian ventures that derive from abstract principles and call for taking extreme steps either have proved impracticable or, when forcefully tried, end in totalitarian societies far worse than the shadowy, muddled, but warmly human, life in the cave. So perhaps under most circumstances, evolutionary rather than revolutionary steps garner better and more secure results. Establishing an academy that nurtures both the body and the mind of the young, as Plato did, is a good start. More than two millennia later, we have no sounder solution than the setting up of schools where the seeds of knowledge, including most importantly the sort that helps citizens decide which institutions and customs to respect and conserve and which to alter or radically change, are planted.

Human Relations in Society

A common criticism against large societies, especially modern society, is that it lacks the warmth of small communities. Human relations are cool and contractual rather than intense. But intensity, we have noted, is not always desirable. There is the intensity of hatred as of love; and even today violence and abuse are more commonplace within the family—within the home—than outside it, on the streets, among strangers.[23] What is desirable in human warmth, then, is not just a level of emotion, but a quality of emotion. And that quality is, to a far larger degree than we realize, a product of reflective and imaginative thinking. Nature sets the juices flowing between (say) man and woman, parent and child, then culture takes over; and the resources of culture—the means by which the imagination enriches even the most basic biological urges—are greater in a literate, technologically advanced society (civilization) than in a small community. This is the heterodox view—heterodox in our own curious time—that I wish to present.

MAN AND WOMAN: EROTIC RELATIONS

Lust, an uncontrollable engorgement of the sexual organs, leads to sweaty bodies coupling compulsively in the dark. One can hardly have a more stark picture of human animality. Too often,

that is all there is: an act that for all its physical intimacy is solip-
sistic in its single-minded concern to find release from tension for
the self. Human cultures try to inject imagination into the act,
transforming the sexual bond into an erotic relationship, into a
social union of families, and even into a cosmic drama uniting the
male and female principles of the universe. Cultures differ in the
degree to which they have sought to explore the subtleties and va-
rieties, the heights and depths, of erotic love. They also differ in
the retention of what they have learned. Here literate cultures enjoy an advantage: what was learned in the past, even in the distant
past, is retained in poems and stories to inspire the present. Young
Iranians today, hiding in the hills from the disapproving eyes of
the mullahs, find ways to express their love for each other in
models provided by the eleventh-century Persian poet Omar
Khayyam: thus a young woman in flowing tresses and white
denim sits under a tree, shelling pistachio nuts and dropping
them into the mouth of a young man whose head is in her lap.[24]
Western youngsters are fortunate in that they are inheritors of an
extraordinary range of romantic and erotic literature of the highest caliber, which they can use to convert the raw throbs of the
body into grand human passions, sacred and profane.[25]

PARENT AND CHILD: THE FAMILY

The love of parents for their offspring is natural, as natural as the
sexual attraction between man and woman. Yet, in both Western
and Eastern civilizations, parent-child love has not been celebrated
in great works of literature and music to anything like the same extent as has erotic love. The reason is this: Artworks have always been,
in varying degree, subversive of society, the foundation of which is
the family, the natural bond between parent and child. This bond is

supported by immemorial custom, moral admonitions, and the law. It has no need of imaginative flights, nor does it stimulate them. By contrast, erotic passion does stimulate the imagination, and all the more so if it becomes a symbol of mystical-transcendental longings that can radically subvert social norms.

Erotic love, above a certain level of intensity, threatens the hearth: lovers leap over its walls to be with each other and to be in a larger, more tolerant world. Parent-child love, by contrast, is of the essence of the hearth. And perhaps for this reason, its warmth is often most evident in small, "primitive" communities, where one may see a young child tied to its mother's back for hours at a stretch as she does her daily chores, or a boy and his father engaged in play that is also—to the boy—a preparation for adult life. In civilized societies, the natural affection between parent (especially father) and child is too often overlain by an impersonal authoritarian structure of power. Here would seem to be an example of how a fundamental human relationship cools when the scale of society becomes too large and complex. Yet appearances can be deceiving. The affection may be buried, but it is there. We are little aware of it because it is seldom expressed in writing, except as spontaneous comments in private correspondence or diaries that are unlikely to survive. The few that do survive show how tender feelings rooted in nature and in the hearth can remain much the same even as the outward social forms of family change in major ways.[26]

A happy turn of events in modern times is the decline of patriarchy and, along with it, a resurfacing of natural affection between male parent and offspring, a man and his family. Modern fathers not only play with their young children, but feel derelict if they do not also, as a matter of course, make them peanut butter sandwiches or wipe their noses. In the midst of cosmopolitan life, there is the hearth, the family—a modern Eden that only the most cynical would call a total illusion. I am struck by a letter that the great mathematician-philosopher Alfred North Whitehead wrote to his son North on December 10, 1924. After first saying that he could imagine his grandchildren growing up by predictable stages, he added that, looking back on life, he would consider bringing up a family "by far the achievement most worth while":

I don't mean solely the production of individuals one loves devotedly—of course that is immense. But in the recollection of it, when life holds so much that is recollection, there is a colour and meaning in the retrospect even of the most anxious moments which relieves life of a sense of barrenness which I have often noticed damping elderly people who have never had such intimate jobs.[27]

Whitehead reminds us that much of life—certainly much of life's savor—is recollection. Stories help parents to recollect. All parents like to tell stories of their children. Modern parents, however, have the advantage of being able to weave their tales around snapshots in the family album. Photographs are not only reminders of persons and events in all their concrete specificity; they *are* bits of reality from the past—a child's shape and gesture, a stubby toy shovel, imposing themselves on sensitive film—that can endlessly stimulate a fond viewer's imagination. What does it mean to know someone else? It means, at a minimum, seeing that person clearly, in detail. Corrective lenses (spectacles) help: how easily we take them for granted, as though they were a natural given rather than the invention of a particular time! And snapshots help— snapshots that wondrously collapse time, fusing the toddler's dimpled grin with the young man or woman standing before us today. Technology, not just sonnets and stories, adds warmth and depth to human relationships, a theme that is curiously neglected in scholarly writings.

CARING FOR OTHERS

One reason for our deep attachment to the hearth is that it is where we receive care when we are sick. The human species is unique among primates in having a hearth (home) in that sense. Since earliest times, a sick person stays at home to be looked after, while others move out to forage and hunt. No such base exists among baboons, other monkeys, apes. As an anthropologist puts it, "When the troop moves out on the daily round, *all* members must move with it or be deserted. The only protection for the baboon is to stay with the troop, no matter how injured or sick he may be. . . . For a wild primate a fatal sickness is one that separates it from the troop, but for man it is one from which he cannot recover even while protected and fed at the home base."[28]

Human attachment is not, of course, just to a particular place; it is as much, or even more, to the people who discern one's distress and seek to alleviate it. Who are these people? Since time immemorial, they are one's kin, closest neighbors, and possibly other members of one's own group. But they will not be strangers. The parable of the Good Samaritan was remarkable for its time, as it is even today, because help that required considerable expenditure of energy and money was extended to a wounded stranger lying by the side of a public road. In tribal and folk communities, it is assumed that charity not only begins but should end at home: mutual regard and helpfulness within the group are combined with an almost utter indifference to the fate of outsiders. Consider imperial China. Although numerically a country of illiterate peasants, it was not a folk society. Imperial China boasted not only cosmopolitan sophistication but high social ideals, which included the duty to protect the common people against natural disaster by installing flood control systems and public granaries. Yet imperial China retained one folk trait, namely, the unquestioned primacy of family and kinsfolk. Confucianism itself, though it urged universal benignity, assumed that one should devote oneself first to family. Significantly, it was not Confucianism but a foreign universal religion—Buddhism—that introduced into China (around the fifth century) public institutions of charity such as hospitals, almshouses, dispensaries, and centers for the distribution of aid to the poor.[29] In the Western world, again it was a religion that recognized no distinction between Jew and Greek and preached the example of the Good Samaritan that built inns for travelers and hospitals for the poor; and, significantly, these homes were first established in the eleventh and twelfth centuries, not through the initiatives of the church hierarchy, but through the preaching and example of rootless hermits.[30]

A sense of obligation to strangers—even to those who live on the other side of the ocean—has come to be taken for granted in Western countries, part of their middle-class family's hoary chest of morals, aired from time to time for the benefit of the young. Yet, if we pause to think, we realize that helping strangers with no expectation of a return is in fact a sophisticated and hence rather unnatural frame of mind. In Western Europe or North America, a child who fails to eat everything on her plate is told, "Think of the starving millions in China [India, or Ethiopia]!" The child may well respond, "But why should I think about them when, so far as I know, they do not think about me?" And if she is precocious, she might add, "There has to be reciprocity in any human relationship, you know." Parents may be hard put to give an adequate response because they have learned to assume that some stirring of conscience, some gesture of help, is called for wherever severe suffering is known to have occurred. This concern for the welfare of total strangers is uniquely developed in the West. Even in the 1980s and 1990s, starvation and sickness in an African country are more likely to arouse the sympathy of ordinary Western Europeans and North Americans, who may send a check or volunteer their services, than of Africans in neighboring states.[31] Difference in economic means cannot be the sole answer, for if so, what about the affluent Japanese? Their middle-class people do not feel any obligation to dispatch missions to foreign countries ravaged by epidemics. It is not their tradition. And if they are beginning to extend such help in recent years, it is because they, in this matter too, have come under the influence of the West.

Recovering at home under the care of family and kinfolk enhances one's warm feeling toward family and home. The care that is received will be returned, if not immediately in similar care, then in tokens of appreciation and deference. Such reciprocity is at the heart of traditional familial and communal bonds. Now consider a different picture—recovering in a public hospital surrounded and nurtured by strangers, nurses who remove one's bedpan, doctors who check one's chart on their midnight rounds. How is one to feel toward them and toward the hospital itself?

Circular Reciprocity and Generosity

The small traditional community, dependent on the vagaries of nature, is a community of toil. Romanticizing it, calling it the true community (as Martin Buber has done), is tempting if only because reciprocity is there a rule of life. We have noted, however, that this reciprocity operates under the constraint of dire need. Peasant farmers have to help one another to survive; moreover, they know that they must ladle out their help in a calculating manner. "My Father and my mother have sent you a Pudding and a Chine, and desire you when you kill your Hogges, you will send him as good again," says a seventeenth-century farmer.[32] A narrowly understood reciprocity is the common practice: hard-pressed villagers cannot even pretend to be generous. Yet the desire to be so may well be there. Wherever a margin of surplus is the norm, generosity insinuates itself into customs of exchange. In small-town America, for instance, neighbors try to give a little more than they take—giving back two cups of vinegar for the one cup taken, or returning tools shinier than they were when borrowed.

The existence of a surplus means that villagers can go to the market to barter, or sell and buy. In contrast to exchanges among neighbors within the village, which are strictly practical and rather joyless, trips to the market can be happy occasions. One source of happiness is the sense of release from agricultural toil and from the community's tight social rules. The journey to the market is itself a liberating experience. Another source of happiness is that villagers anticipate being somewhat richer when they return—richer materially, in friendships, and in knowledge of a larger world. At the market, which is mostly filled with acquaintances and strangers, they can afford to be more open and generous, dispensing friendly touches, shouts of greeting, even token pieces of merchandise, without incurring complex reciprocal debts and obligations.

The awareness of "What's in it for me?" is reduced if instead of a narrow reciprocity, people engage in what Lewis Hyde calls "circular" giving. A gives to B who gives to C who gives to D who gives to A.[33] Generosity is eventually recompensed but only after a long delay, and it will not come from the individual to whom one has given. The larger and more complex the society the more likely its people are to practice circular giving that draws in not only friends and acquaintances but total strangers. In a modern society, the circle of giving may be so large that it cannot be encompassed by direct experience. What occurs seems linear—a long line that extends into a distant future inhabited by strangers. Modern parents, for example, care for their children with little expectation of material return; their children will in time care for their own offspring, and so on down the line. Other human relationships may show a similar linearity. A social worker helps someone who, perhaps out of gratitude, helps someone else. The favor one does is not returned. One's action does not necessarily gain one a friend or an ally; indeed, the recipient of one's largesse may never be seen again.[34]

In modern society, good Samaritanship is commonplace. The help we extend to the stranger may not amount to much: it may merely be some service to a customer. Yet even there, in many professions, a measure of heroism—an extra giving of self—is almost routine: thus the teacher patiently quiets down a thrashing, hyperactive child, the bus driver helps oldsters in wheelchairs in and out of his specially equipped vehicle all day, the medic applies mouth-to-mouth resuscitation to a man who has just vomited, the firefighters plunge into a burning house to save people they do not know. If we ask the firefighters, "Why do you do it?" the answer is likely to be a shrug and, "Oh, it's a job." The casualness of that response says something eloquent about society. True, there is the money nexus: we pay and are paid for these and other services, but the relation between the amount of pay and the service rendered is seldom commensurate or clear. One thing *is* clear: the amount we pay is necessarily very little compared with the goods and services received. What we receive at a department store, an art museum, in an ambulance or a hospital is the *cumulated* labor, skill, and knowledge of a long trail of total strangers, most of whom are dead.

If any people should be ancestor worshipers, it is modern people. More generally, the people of any historic civilization, as inheritors of highly tangible achievements (from wheeled vehicles that facilitate transportation to lanterns that illumine the night), have special reason to be grateful. Historic consciousness incurs a sense of gratitude to the past, which translates into an attitude of concern for, and generosity toward, the future. Narrow reciprocity is an arrangement of convenience in the present among individuals who know one another. Circular reciprocity and linear giving, by contrast, stretch out time into past, present, and future, and with such stretching more and more people—more and more strangers, historically as well as spatially—are drawn into a vast net of debt and obligation.

From Communal Singing to Conversation

Community is a warm nurturing place, an Eden that we have lost. Although I have cast doubt on the actual existence of such a place and in particular questioned the idealized image of human relationships in it, I would now like to add that in one sense this "warmth" did exist among people in simpler times, a warmth that we in modern society seldom experience. It is the warmth of total belongingness. One feels it most in communal singing. People get together, feel together—indeed, feel as *one*—when they sing. That is its deepest purpose. People sing essentially to themselves. There are no listeners; there is no human audience "out there." The welling up of emotion—drenched, rhythmic sound—swallows up the individual singer, makes him or her a part of the whole to a degree that no other group activity can. Working together at a common task no doubt also creates a strong sense of oneness, but, significantly, that oneness is enhanced by work songs, which enable laborers to forget their own fatigue in their total identification with the group.

Human oneness is not, however, all that transpires when people sing. If this oneness were all that people desire, then wordless songs would serve the purpose. But words are always linked to tones in a song. Why? Victor Zuckerkandl's answer is that words have the power to connect a person with the world, that is with *things* as well as with the human group. If only words are used, the link between person and things remains rather cool and distant: the things remain "outside" the person. When words are not only spoken but sung, they somehow can establish an emotional bond between person and things, breaking down the distinction and the separateness.[35]

Community is communication, and a unique form of human communication is speech. People sit around a meal, a fire, or just a patch of ground. Currents of words move back and forth, weaving individual speakers into a whole. This is a human universal: what our most distant ancestors did, we still do—everywhere. What is being communicated? Nothing much, irrespective of the intelligence and learning of the participants. Social talk consists almost entirely of inconsequential gossip, brief accounts of the experiences and events of the day. A corollary of that inconsequentiality is that no one really listens. When, by chance, two persons are drawn into a real conversation, the host considers it his duty to break it up so as to reintegrate them into the group.

Communal singing (without external audience) appears to be largely a thing of the past. Social talk is, of course, still very much with us: it too welds participants into one whole, though less strongly and seamlessly than in communal singing. Distinct from talk is conversation. And I would like to argue that conversation is characteristic of complex societies, and especially of modern society. Conversation occurs when a serious attempt is made to explore "self" and "world" with another.[36] It presupposes an awareness of self in all its elusive complexity and depth, which in turn implies the existence of private space (one's own room, one's own collection of books) to which one can withdraw to think and meditate. It presupposes, further, a degree of sociopsychological independence from the group and its pressures, and a willingness to listen to another even though he may not come cloaked in formal authority. Conversation, as distinct from talk and admonition, rarely takes place within the family—certainly not in a tradition-bound family. It is typically something that happens between strangers who, as a result of such interaction, become friends. Conversation may occur in the home, but more often than not, it occurs in public space—on a park bench, on a country lane, in a tavern or coffee shop. The impersonal public space encourages individuals to be more themselves, freed from the thick atmosphere of kinship and family (all those pictures of children on the mantelpiece) that a home inevitably exudes. Conversation, then, is an accomplishment of the cosmos rather than of the hearth. If it does take place at the hearth, between husband and wife (for instance), it is evidence that the hearth has been infiltrated by the cosmos.

Conversation between friends tends to be an even balance between the topic of "self" and the topic of "world." It need not be egocentric even when the topic is the self, for to speak of the self competently one must also speak of its environment, which in the largest sense is the world. When, however, the world is the sole subject of conversation, it becomes something that transpires between colleagues—fellow scholars and scientists—rather than between friends. We may thus speak of a general conversation between friends and a specialized conversation between colleagues. Anyone can turn out to be an enthusiast for the American Constitution, Chinese porcelain, butterflies, inorganic chemistry, whatever. And that enthusiasm, combined with real knowledge, is the only condition for colleagueship. People with a common interest meet in a public place to read papers to one another, to converse. They form learned societies. Many such societies were established in the eighteenth century, including several in America. Since 1800, professional societies of all kinds in every conceivable area of learning have multiplied beyond measure. Unlike professional guilds of the past, which were devoted to passing on practical knowledge and skills, modern societies are primarily places for the exchange of ideas—for specialized conversation. And, again, unlike professional guilds of the past, which tightly monitored membership and favored kinsmen, modern societies are (at least in their best moments) open to all who have the necessary talent and qualifications.

Friends and colleagues, the one private, the other public, have much in common. Both flourish in a cosmopolitan world. Both are open-ended: one can have many colleagues, and one can have more than one close friend. In both types of relationships, commonality and difference, and the fruitful tension between them, are accepted and indeed welcomed. When friends and colleagues meet, their purpose is not to seek oneness as in communal singing, or togetherness as in social chitchat, but rather participation in the discovery of a deeper truth, a larger reality. Friends need to withdraw from each other periodically in order to be more themselves, in order that their individualities—their differences—can grow. The differences are, as it were, gifts that they bring to the meeting. The same can be said about the dynamics of colleagueship. In a large scientific meeting, for example, people from all parts of the world congregate to share what they have learned in relative isolation—that is, in their own countries, their own laboratories, among members of their own team. Friends and colleagues delight in their different experiences and experiments—in their temporary separation—because they can always look forward to coming together again, and because they do, after all, share a common purpose.

Encompassing Vision versus Diversity

A diversity of hearths is itself a cosmopolitan ideal. To people who have never ventured beyond their homeplace and to people who withdraw into it in fear as to a besieged fortress, diversity—the plenitude of the great world—is a threat. Curiously, cosmos itself can be such a fortress, for however bold and imaginative the original spirit is, it may in time falter, become anxious, to the extent of turning its own dream and creation into a rigid structure, a stronghold that is little better than a capacious and stylishly furnished prison. To be a viable ideal, then, cosmos needs the joint inspiration of its two models: simplifying vision and plenitude. The one exalts the human spirit, lifting it from bondage to a particular time and place through conceptual and technological leaps; the other anchors that spirit in the tumult and fecundity of empirical facts.

Historically, at a philosophical-scientific level, the West has shown an enduring interest in both models since classical antiquity. In America (as I have noted in chapter 3), it was manifest in the conflict between two academies—Boston's and Philadelphia's—the one stressing Newtonian astronomy and mathematics, the other the plenitude of nature. At a sociopolitical level, in the early years of the republic, an analogous split existed between, on the one hand, the desire for probity and virtue modeled on republican Rome, and, on the other hand, the willingness to experiment in a form of government and society that could accommodate and be enriched by immigrants of diverse backgrounds. This split is discernible throughout American history, although the ways in which these two components ("unum" and "pluribus") are conceived have changed. During the first half of the twentieth century, the United States, confidently united, believed that progress toward a modern and just world could only come under the aegis of "democracy" and "science." America led the world in "democracy" and "science"—in the march toward modernization. Other countries would follow.

Near the end of the twentieth century, the twin banners of "democracy" and "science" continue to fly. No other worldwide vision challenges that twofold ideal. More and more countries aspire to be modern—that is, in some sense, "democratic" and empowered by the lucidities and material benefits of science. On the other hand, the banners are no longer flying proudly, as they did in the first half of the century. Doubts have arisen, not only among those who failed to move up the ladder of modernization and into cosmopolitan society (and they are many in the world and in the United States itself), but also among thinking people who are themselves cosmopolitans. These privileged opinionmakers fall into two groups. One group denounces modernism as a hegemonic ideology, somehow linked to imperialism, that has trampled on the world's diverse cultures, each of which has been a nurturing hearth to a people. The second group openly acknowledges its cosmopolite-cosmopolitan background; and while it still owes allegiance to its Enlightenment heritage, including dreams of progress, it would like to see the thrust of progress—and of modernism—modulate into something more temperate, slowed down by ironic skeptical thought and the sheer weight of multitudinous facts, into high modernism.

Concerning the first group's attitude and posture, two things stand out as wrong—one moral, the other practical. It is unconscionable for anyone who enjoys the advantages of cosmopolitan life to tell those who lack material resources and are constricted in mobility that they should stay home, embedded in their culture—be one specimen among others in the world's *cabinet de curiosités*, a source of satisfaction to the cosmopolitan curator or tourist. The moral calculus alters if the people themselves seek withdrawal behind protective barriers. Here the objection is one of practicality: in today's world it is not practical for an ethnic group, from a sense of hurt and cultural pride, to fully withdraw from the larger society; it is neither practical nor desirable, for most people nowadays want access to running water, electricity, and perhaps antibiotics and the telephone.

Limits: A High-Modern Cosmos

Men and women of the second group, those who openly acknowledge their cosmopolite-cosmopolitan background, continue to be inspired by the possibilities of a modern and just world. They differ from ambitious modernists of an earlier period in having a strong sense of limits and limitations, derived in part from experience, in part from a more reflective and skeptical mode of thinking. This return to a less Faustian outlook on what human beings can achieve differentiates "high modern" from "modern."

What do I mean by limits and limitations? Science itself is the study of constraints and limits in nature; and these, when precisely formulated, are called laws. Laws dictate the motion of the stars, the direction of streamflow, the distribution and evolution of plants and animals, species emergences and extinctions, population explosions and crashes. A characteristic of the late twentieth century—of high modernism—is the awareness that human beings are not exempt from these laws, that the hubris of modernism, which is not only having but *rushing into* megaprojects, can lead to disaster. Geographers, like many environmentalists and informed citizens, are aware of limitations on this global scale, but they are just as keenly aware of it at the scale of the earth's myriad landscapes, which they see as the working out of human and nonhuman forces. A landscape is a small unit of the earth on which a people have come to depend for both their live-lihood and their sense of well-being. Streets and houses testify to human force, yet at every point they can be understood as regis-tering and responding to natural forces: the roofs slanted to shed snow, the windows facing west for a view of the beach, the streets potholed following each spring thaw, sizzling summer heat that imparts an extra friendliness to the bells of the ice cream van, and so on—details that people barely remember but that are inscribed in their lives and that, if absent, can be sorely missed.[37]

The philosopher Leszek Kolakowski writes: "When I am asked where I would like to live, my standard answer is: deep in the vir-gin mountain forest on a lake shore at the corner of Madison Av-enue in Manhattan and Champs-Elysées, in a small tidy town."[38] Thus speaks a cosmopolitan, but even more a person who is not really at home anywhere, for the place he wants to live in not only does not exist but cannot exist—it is contradictory. Most people, however, will identify with one landscape, often the one that they have grown up in, a patch of the earth soaked with childhood in-toxications in which every newly gained taste, habit, or value in-timately meshes with a particular object or setting. Visits to exotic places later in life can bring excitement and pleasure, but they can also raise people's conscious awareness of their deep attachment to home. It may even be that one true benefit of exploration is "to arrive where [they] started / And know the place for the first time" (T. S. Eliot).[39]

Culture, I have noted earlier, limits experience and focuses attention, thereby imparting a vividness and intensity (value) to what is experienced and focused on. Without such constraints and bounds, human beings are adrift. Cosmopolitans, viewed positively as I have done in this book, are a people in love with the splendor and plenitude of life. Viewed negatively, they are a people adrift, flitting from one thing to another (language, idea, place, people, custom) with no point of enduring rest and hence no deep knowledge or commitment. A cosmopolitan place, again viewed negatively, is a "flea market" (to use Boris Pasternak's condemnatory term) of gaudy, cheap, imitative wares, and anxious, frantic people striving for the cheap thrill and material advantage.[40] By contrast, culture, with its taboos, provides anchorage in a warmly human hearth or landscape. Have I, then, reversed my position, lauding culture whereas earlier I had been critical? Not at all. Culture, with its exclusivity and excess burden of taboos, remains problematic. What I would now like to do is to introduce a revised conception of culture, one that has the coziness but not the narrowness and bigotry of the traditional hearth. I shall call it, paradoxically, "cosmopolitan hearth."

Cosmopolitan Hearth

The world is still rich in cultures and landscapes, though their number is diminishing and their signal traits are fading. What should we do? Some steps that have been envisaged, advocated, or put into practice include preservationism—that is, attempting to preserve human culture as though it were a form of endangered wildlife; cultural-ethnic chauvinism; religious fundamentalism; and returning to an imagined rustic or small-town past. These are not the steps favored by high modernism. What then does it favor? What does it envisage? Consider the expression "cosmopolitan hearth." The emphasis is on "hearth" rather than on "cosmopolitan" in recognition of a fundamental fact about human beings, which is that free spirits—true cosmopolites—whose emotional center or home is a mystical religion or philosophy, an all-consuming art or science, are few in number and always will be. The binding powers of culture are nearly inexorable: note that even the most highly educated people (the Bloomsbury literati, for example) can be as narrowly bound to a particular culture (English country house and afternoon teas), as xenophobic and intolerant of what they don't know, as the provincials and primitive folks they disdain.[41] So we are all more or less hearth-bound. We can, however, make a virtue of necessity. We can learn to appreciate intelligently our culture and landscape.

"Intelligently" is the word to underline. What does it mean in practice? A modest beginning would be to know the local geography, but this should include lived experience and not just impersonal facts. We need to remember how it is to wake up in the middle of the night to the crash of hail on the roof and feel, because the blanket has migrated up to our shoulders, the chill of exposed feet. Knowing places other than our own is a necessary component of the concept of "cosmopolitan hearth." The unique personality of our small part of the earth is all the more real and precious when we can compare it with other climes, other topographies. Perhaps this is another way of saying that exploration (moving out into the cosmos) enables us to know our own hearth better—indeed, "for the first time." Difference contributes to self-awareness, and that is one reason why high modernism is in favor of difference. But, curiously, awareness of commonality, rather than destroying local distinction, can subtly add to it by giving it greater weight. In a rowboat on Lake Mendota, in Madison, Wisconsin, I look at the moon. The same moon will one night enthrall someone in a rowboat on Lake Como, Italy. I do not feel diminished by sharing the moon with an Italian, nor does Lake Mendota seem less unique.

The next step is to get a firm grip on our own culture—the custom or habit that, stamped on habitat, produces a homeplace. If it is difficult to appraise habitat with the fresh and eager eyes of a visitor, it is more difficult to appraise—or even be aware of—habits, especially those that we repeat daily. I think here not only of such larger acts as getting out of bed, going to the bathroom, preparing and eating breakfast, and so on through the day, but also the infinite number of miniacts within them, such as how one squeezes the toothpaste tube, eats peas, pats the dog, smells the evening air. Miniacts (habits) have their own minihabitats, and these are even more likely to escape our conscious awareness. The recognition that living as such, in all its detail and density, is a terra incognita that eludes scientific probing is an instance of high-modern sensibility. One consequence is the wish to protect the warm core of living, so vulnerable in its inarticulateness, from aggressive rationality and modernism.

Distinct from habits and routines are celebrations and rituals that, although they are recurrent, recur after a sufficient lapse of time to seem new; in any case, they are intended to be occasions of heightened awareness. Such special occasions may be either personal-familial or public. In the first category are births, weddings, funerals; in the second are rituals that punctuate the agricultural calendar or memorialize historic events. They are all supported by an appropriate stage, special costumes, decorations, artworks, perhaps music. Each event is thus a large chunk of culture on display. For this reason, when people want to rehabilitate their culture, they often think of resurrecting a traditional festival or ritual. Many communities in the United States, fighting the homogenizing forces of modernization, turn to ethnic roots for significant markers of difference. Some communal leaders take this returning to roots with great seriousness, for in their minds it is also a way of regaining a lost sense of collective self and authenticity. Nevertheless, in at least the well-to-do American communities (as distinct from Buber's communities of toil and tribulation), what actually happens is that a people at play or engaged in display act out their "pasts" with varying degrees of self-consciousness and irony.[42]

Without modernism, there cannot be high modernism. Modernism provides the necessary security, which includes material sufficiency, social-institutional safety nets such as insurance and government subsidies, and, thanks to science, substantial freedom from the vagaries of nature and almost total exemption from the dread of dark magic, ghosts, witches, and demons. Against this background of security, communities can selectively re-create the past. None seeks to resurrect the old insecurities and fears. If an old custom is re-created, it is more likely to be a birthday or wedding than a funeral. As for agricultural rites, late-twentieth-century versions, even if they are correct in every historical-factual detail, cannot recapture the mood of helplessness and dread that drove people to practice animal and even (if one goes back far enough) human sacrifice. Another major difference is this. In the past, festivals and rituals were conducted primarily for local consumption, to establish some sort of harmony between people and nature. By contrast, in the late twentieth century, although festivals continue to promote communality and a sense of place, as much or even more are they set up to attract benign strangers. The local place in our time, far from being indifferent or hostile to the big world, welcomes it. One might say, perhaps a touch cynically, that today's reconstituted festivals are intended to propitiate another kind of god (tourists) and induce another kind of blessing (money).

A common criticism leveled against places that try to reinvent their individualized selves is that the results are rather bland and tend not to be sharply differentiated from one another. This criticism reminds me of *Anna Karenina*'s famous opening sentence: "All happy families are like one another; each unhappy family is unhappy in its own way." A lax paraphrase might be to say that ways of showing common decency are limited, whereas ways of showing perversity are not only many but highly colorful, the stuff of popular ethnographies: infanticide, child bride, scarification, bloody rites of animal and human sacrifice, foot binding, self-immolation of widows, demon possession, witch burning, and so on. No doubt the world's cultural diversity suffers as a result of the demise of these practices, but this particular loss can be borne by anyone touched by the spirit of enlightenment. Another reason for the lack of striking differences among the better-off ethnic communities (for instance, those in the United States) is their openness to the world; they were—but are no longer—communities beleaguered by nature and hostile strangers. In the United States, beleaguered communities still exist, either as a consequence of the larger world's persisting intransigence, or because of the group's own desperate need to withdraw, from a sense of past injury and from a present feeling of inadequacy, into defensive enclaves. It is in these enclaves, where no ordinary tourist would want to go, that we are most likely to find cultural exotica.

This last point raises a general question, which not only individuals but communities need to address, namely, how much of the world to keep out so as to allow personal and local virtues to grow that can then be offered to the world, and how much of that world to let in so as to prevent sterility or the development of traits that are pathological or merely eccentric.

At Home in the Cosmos

"Cosmopolitan hearth" is a contradiction in terms and this fact, perhaps, defines our dilemma—a *human* dilemma that has always existed but that becomes more evident as we move from traditional to modern, then high modern. The dilemma is captured by the observation, which George Steiner and others have made, that whereas plants have roots, human beings have feet.[43] Feet make us mobile, but of course we also have minds, a far greater source of instability and uprooting. Consider such utterly commonplace experiences: while we are "here," we can always imagine being "there," and while we live in the present, we can recall the past and envisage the future. Stay in the same place, and we will still have moved inexorably, for the place of adulthood is not the place of childhood even if nothing in it has materially changed. Stages of life are sometimes called a "journey," a figure of speech that again vividly captures the condition of human homelessness. A paradox peculiar to our time and to Americans especially is that "searching for roots," which is intended to make us (Americans) feel more rooted, can itself be uprooting, that is, done at the expense of intimate involvement with place. Rather than immersion in the locality where we now live, our mind and emotion are ever ready to shift to other localities and times, across the Atlantic or Pacific, to ancestral lands remote from direct experience. We can be dismissive of what is right before our eyes—the local McDonald's where our young children wolf down their hamburgers, the city cemetery where our parents were recently buried—in favor of some place at the other end of the globe where distant forebears lived, toiled, and danced.

Singing together, working together against tangible adversaries, melds us into one whole: we become members of the community, embedded in place. By contrast, thinking—especially thinking of the reflective, ironic, quizzical mode, which is a luxury of affluent societies—threatens to isolate us from our immediate group and home. As vulnerable beings who yearn at times for total immersion, to sing in unison (eyes closed) with others of our kind, this sense of isolation—of being a unique individual—can be felt as a deep loss. Thinking, however, yields a twofold gain: although it isolates us from our immediate group it can link us both seriously and playfully to the cosmos—to strangers in other places and times; and it enables us to accept a human condition that we have always been tempted by fear and anxiety to deny, namely, the impermanence of our state wherever we are, our ultimate homelessness. A cosmopolite is one who considers the gain greater than the loss. Having seen something of the splendid spaces, he or she (like Mole) will not want to return, permanently, to the ambiguous safeness of the hearth.

NOTES

1. Two Scales and Autobiography

1. Kenneth Grahame, *The Wind in the Willows* (New York: Heritage Press, 1944), p. 76.

2. James J. Y. Liu, *The Art of Chinese Poetry* (Chicago: University of Chicago Press, 1962), pp. 55–57.

3. Daniel J. Elazar, *The American Mosaic: The Impact of Space, Time, and Culture on American Politics* (Boulder: Westview Press, 1994), pp. 73–98.

4. Edmund Leach, "Glimpses of the Unmentionable in the History of British Social Anthropology," *Annual Review of Anthropology*, 13 (1984), p. 22.

5. The term *high modernism* doesn't yet enjoy anything like the popularity of *postmodernism*. High modernism was explicated by Anthony Giddens in *The Consequences of Modernity* (Stanford: Stanford University Press, 1990), p. 163, and again, more fully, in *Modernity and Self-Identity* (Stanford: Stanford University Press, 1991), especially pp. 27–32. For an alternative criticism of postmodernism, not so much for its deconstructive excesses as for its continuation—in another, seemingly friendlier guise—of Western epistemological domination, see R. Radhakrishnan, "Postmodernism and the Rest of the World," *Organization: Article on Globalization*, 1 (1994), pp. 305–40. I thank Janaki Bakhle for this reference.

2. China

1. Alfred Forke, *The World Conception of the Chinese* (London: Arthur

Probsthain, 1925); Marcel Granet, *La Pensée Chinoise* (Paris: Albin Michel, 1934), especially the section "Le microcosme," pp. 361–88.

2. Nelson I. Wu, *Chinese and Indian Architecture* (New York: Braziller, 1963).

3. Derk Bodde and Clarence Morris, *Law in Imperial China* (Cambridge: Harvard University Press, 1967), pp. 44, 47.

4. Benjamin Schwartz, *The Thought of Ancient China* (Cambridge: Harvard University Press, 1985), pp. 24, 34.

5. Ray Huang, *China: A Macro-History* (Armonk, N.Y.: M. E. Sharpe, 1989), pp. 14–16.

6. A. F. Wright, "Symbolism and Functions: Reflections on Changan and Other Great Cities," *Journal of Asian Studies*, 24 (1965), p. 670; Wu, *Chinese and Indian Architecture*, p. 38.

7. Yi-Fu Tuan, "A Preface to Chinese Cities," in R. P. Beckinsale and J. M. Houston, eds., *Urbanization and Its Problems* (Oxford: Blackwell, 1968), pp. 247–48.

8. Huang, *China: A Macro-History*, p. 32.

9. James Legge, *Confucian Analects* (New York: Paragon Books, 1966), pp. 73, 87, 142.

10. Burton Watson, trans., *Hsun Tzu: Basic Writings* (New York: Columbia University Press, 1963), pp. 109–10.

11. Ibid., p. 89.

12. Howard J. Wechsler, *Offerings of Jade and Silk: Ritual and Symbol in the Legitimation of the T'ang Dynasty* (New Haven: Yale University Press, 1985), p. 29.

13. Ibid., p. 60.

14. Jeffrey F. Meyer, *The Dragons of Tiananmen: Beijing as a Sacred City* (Columbia: University of South Carolina Press, 1991), p. 137.

15. Herbert Fingarette, *Confucius: The Secular and the Sacred* (New York: Harper Torchbooks, 1972).

16. James Fisher, *Zoos of the World* (London: Aldus Books, 1966), pp. 23–43.

17. Quoted in E. R. Hughes, *Two Chinese Poets: Vignettes of Han Life and Thought* (Princeton: Princeton University Press, 1960), p. 27.

18. Derk Bodde, *China's First Unifier* (Leiden: Brill, 1938), pp. 116–17, 163.

19. E. H. Schafer, "The Last Years of Ch'ang-an," *Oriens Extremus*, 10 (1963), pp. 133–79.

20. E. H. Schafer, *Golden Peaches of Samarkand* (Berkeley: University of California Press, 1963), pp. 15, 18.

21. L. Carrington Goodrich, *A Short History of the Chinese People* (New York: Harper & Brothers, 1959), p. 135.

22. Schafer, "The Last Years of Ch'ang-an," p. 138.

23. Owen Lattimore, "Herdsmen, Farmers, Urban Culture," in *Pastoral Production and Society* (Cambridge: Cambridge University Press, 1979), pp. 485–86.

24. Kenneth Ch'en, *Buddhism in China: A Historical Survey* (Princeton: Princeton University Press, 1964), pp. 179, 259.

25. Ibid., p. 279.

26. Ray Huang, *1587, a Year of No Significance: The Ming Dynasty in Decline* (New Haven: Yale University Press, 1981), pp. 7–8.

27. Etienne Balazs, *Chinese Civilization and Bureaucracy* (New Haven: Yale University Press, 1964), p. 69.

28. Arthur Waley, *Chinese Poems* (London: Unwin Books, 1911), p. 161.

29. Balazs, *Chinese Civilization and Bureaucracy*, p. 71.

30. John K. Fairbank, *China: A New History* (Cambridge: Harvard University Press, 1992), pp. 79–81.

31. Myron L. Cohen, "Being Chinese: The Peripheralization of Traditional Identity," *Daedalus*, 120 (Spring 1991), pp. 121–22; see also Lin Yutang, *My Country and My People* (New York: John Day, 1939), pp. 342–44.

32. Cohen, "Being Chinese," pp. 115–16.

33. Helen F. Siu, "Cultural Identity and the Politics of Difference," *Daedalus*, 122 (Spring 1993), p. 23.

34. David Yen-ho Wu, "The Construction of Chinese and Non-Chinese Identities," *Daedalus*, 120 (Spring 1991), p. 169.

35. H. E. Richardson, *A Short History of Tibet* (New York: Dutton, 1962), pp. 28–29; Charles Bell, *The People of Tibet* (Oxford: Oxford University Press, 1928), pp. 11–12.

36. Herold J. Wiens, *China's March toward the Tropics* (Hamden, Conn.: Shoe String Press, 1954), p. 159.

37. Michael Ng-Quinn, "National Identity in Premodern China: Formation and Role Enactment," in Lowell Dittmer and Samuel S. Kim, eds., *China's Quest for National Identity* (Ithaca: Cornell University Press, 1993), p. 54.

38. Wiens, *China's March toward the Tropics*, p. 90.

39. Ibid., p. 202.

40. Yu Yi-tze, *Chung-Kuo T'u-ssu Chih-tu* (Chung-ch'ing, 1944), p. 33; quoted in Wiens, *China's March toward the Tropics*, p. 219.

41. Mark Elvin, "The Inner World of 1830," *Daedalus*, 120 (Spring 1991), pp. 48–49, 55, 57.

42. Fairbank, *China: A New History*, pp. 265–69.

43. Robert B. Ekvall, *Cultural Relations on the Kansu-Tibetan Border*, University of Chicago Publications in Anthropology Occasional Papers no. 1, 1939. I am indebted to Ekvall's research for this comparison of the three cultures.

44. Ibid., pp. 44–45.

45. Ibid., p. 46.

46. Ibid., p. 20.

47. Ibid., p. 22.

48. Ibid., p. 21.

49. Ibid., pp. 22–23.

50. Ibid., p. 23.

51. Ibid., pp. 24–25.

52. Ibid., pp. 77–79.

53. Dru C. Gladney, "Representing Nationality in China: Refiguring Majority/Minority Identities," *Journal of Asian Studies*, 53 (1994), pp. 92–123.

54. Thomas Heberer, *China and Its National Minorities: Autonomy or Assimilation?* (Armonk, N.Y.: M. E. Sharpe, 1989), pp. 25–29.

55. The Blacks (Chuanqing) of Kuei-chou applied for minority status so that they could be protected from their neighbors the Blues, but the Blacks were in fact Han. See Heberer, ibid., pp. 36–37. The Bai of Yunnan, who once proudly claimed to be Han, later chose to acknowledge their minority status because of the official policy of giving certain socioeconomic advantages to minorities. See Wu, "The Construction of Chinese and Non-Chinese Identities," p. 171.

56. Peter Bishop, *The Myth of Shangri-la* (Berkeley and Los Angeles: University of California Press, 1989).

57. Heinrich Harrer, *Seven Years in Tibet* (New York: Dutton Paperbacks, 1959), pp. 169-70; on prayer wheel technology, see Lynn White Jr., "Tibet, India, and Malaya as Sources of Western Medieval Technology," *American Historical Review*, 65 (1960), pp. 515–26.

58. H. E. Richardson, *A Short History of Tibet*, pp. 14–17; Pedro Carrasco, *Land and Polity in Tibet* (Seattle: University of Washington Press, 1959), pp.

28, 100–101; R. A. Stein, *Tibetan Civilization* (Stanford: Stanford University Press, 1972), pp. 92–138.

59. Harrer, *Seven Years in Tibet*, p. 176.

60. Ibid., p. 171.

61. Ibid., p. 204. For the influence of Indian Tantrism and Bon on Lamaism, see Stein, *Tibetan Civilization*, pp. 190–91.

62. Richardson, *A Short History of Tibet*, p. 192. The full-scale assault on Tibetan culture and society is described in Pierre-Antoine Donnet, *Tibet: Survival in Question* (Delhi: Oxford University Press, 1994).

63. Jeremy Bernstein, "A Journey to Lhasa," *New Yorker*, December 14, 1987, p. 95.

64. Ibid., p. 99.

65. Ibid., p. 101.

66. Ying-shih Yu, "The Radicalization of China in the Twentieth Century," *Daedalus*, 122 (Spring 1993), pp. 136–39.

67. Ibid., p. 141.

68. Samuel S. Kim and Lowell Dittmer, "Whither China's Quest for National Identity?" in Dittmer and Kim, *China's Quest for National Identity*, pp. 265–67.

69. Gladney, "Representing Nationality in China."

70. Schafer, *Golden Peaches of Samarkand*, pp. 15, 18; E. A. Kracke, "Sung Society: Change within Tradition," *Far Eastern Quarterly*, 14 (1955), pp. 481–82; A. C. Moule, *Quinsai* (Cambridge: Cambridge University Press, 1957), p. 12.

71. Lynn White and Li Cheng, "China's Coastal Identities: Regional, National, and Global," in Dittmer and Kim, *China's Quest for National Identity*, pp. 154–93.

72. Edward Friedman, "Reconstructing China's National Identity: A Southern Alternative to Mao-Era Anti-Imperialist Nationalism," *Journal of Asian Studies*, 53 (1994), pp. 67–91.

3. The United States

1. Leslie Fiedler, *The Return of the Vanishing American* (New York: Stein & Day, 1968), pp. 16–22.

2. Loren Baritz, "The Idea of the West," *American Historical Review*, 66 (1961), pp. 618–40.

3. Jonathan Edwards, *Thoughts on the Revival of Religion in New England, 1740* (New York: n.d.), pp. 196–97; quoted by Baritz, ibid., p. 637.

4. C. Gregory Crampton and Gloria Griffin, "The San Buenaventura, Mythical River of the West," *Mississippi Valley Historical Review*, 25 (1956), pp. 163–71.

5. Quoted by Baritz, "The Idea of the West," pp. 636, 637.

6. Ibid., pp. 638, 639.

7. Daniel J. Boorstin, *Hidden History: Exploring Our Secret Past* (New York: Vintage, 1989), pp. 86–87; William Cronon, George Miles, and Jay Gitlin, "Becoming West: Toward a New Meaning for Western History," in Cronon, Miles, and Gitlin, eds., *Under an Open Sky: Rethinking America's Western Past* (New York: Norton, 1992), pp. 3–27.

8. Perry Miller, *Errand into Wilderness* (New York: Harper Torchbooks, 1964), pp. 211-12.

9. Howard Mumford Jones, *O Strange New World* (New York: Viking Press, 1964), pp. 35–70.

10. Francis Parkman, *Works* (Boston, 1897–98), vol. 18, pp. 119–20. Quoted by Jones, ibid., pp. 370–71.

11. Jack P. Greene, *Intellectual Construction of America: Exceptionalism and Identity from 1492 to 1800* (Chapel Hill: University of North Carolina Press, 1993), pp. 24, 117; Norbert Elias, *The Civilizing Process: The History of Manners* (New York: Urizen Books, 1978).

12. William Currie, *Historical Account of the Climate and Diseases of the United States of America . . .* (Philadelphia, 1792), pp. 408–9; quoted by Henry Steele Commager, *The Empire of Reason: How Europe Imagined and America Realized the Enlightenment* (Garden City, N.Y.: Anchor Press/Doubleday, 1977), p. 101.

13. Boorstin, *Hidden History*, pp. 171, 186–89.

14. Hildegard Binder Johnson, *The Orderly Landscape: Landscape Tastes and the United States Survey*. James Ford Bell Lectures, no. 15 (Minneapolis: University of Minnesota, 1977); Robert David Sack, *Human Territoriality: Its Theory and History* (Cambridge: Cambridge University Press, 1986), pp. 144–63.

15. J. B. Jackson, *Discovering the Vernacular Landscape* (New Haven: Yale University Press, 1984), p. 67.

16. Commager, *The Empire of Reason*, pp. 127–28.

17. Boorstin, *Hidden History*, pp. 306–7.

18. Henry F. May, *The Enlightenment in America* (New York: Oxford University Press, 1976), p. 89.

19. Thomas Paine, "Common Sense," in *Complete Writings*, ed. Philip S. Foner (New York: 1945), vol. 1, p. 3; quoted in May, ibid., p. 163.

20. Perry Miller, *The Life of the Mind in America: From the Revolution to the Civil War* (New York: Harcourt, Brace & World, 1965), pp. 13, 22, 45–47.

21. Ibid., p. 52.

22. Greene, *Intellectual Construction of America*, pp. 24, 35, 48, 93, 117; "some tribes of naked and miserable savages," Adam Smith, *The Nature and Causes of the Wealth of Nations*, in the Glasgow Edition of the *Works and Correspondence of Adam Smith*, ed. R. H. Campbell and A. S. Skinner, 6 vols. (Oxford, 1976–83), vol. 2, p. 559.

23. May, *Enlightment in America*, pp. 134–35, 149.

24. Durand Echeverria, ed., "Condorcet's *The Influence of the American Revolution on Europe*," *William and Mary Quarterly*, 3rd ser., vol. 25 (1968), pp. 95–96; quoted in Greene, *Intellectual Construction of America*, pp. 144–45.

25. Greene, *Intellectual Construction of America*, p. 154.

26. Linda Kerber, *Federalists in Dissent: Imagery and Ideology in Jeffersonian America* (Ithaca: Cornell University Press, 1970), pp. 67–69, 77–79, 93.

27. Ibid., pp. 201–2.

28. Edwin T. Martin, *Thomas Jefferson, Scientist* (New York, 1952), p. 47.

29. May, *Enlightenment in America*, pp. 274–76.

30. Quoted in Boorstin, *Hidden History*, p. 182.

31. May, *Enlightenment in America*, p. 30.

32. St. John de Crèvecoeur, *Letters from an American Farmer* (New York: E. P. Dutton, 1957), pp. 44, 46–47.

33. Miller, *The Life of the Mind in America*, p. 45.

34. Ibid., p. 70.

35. Boorstin, *Hidden History*, p. 88.

36. Michael Walzer, *What It Means to Be an American: Essays on the American Experience* (New York: Marsilio, 1992).

37. Greene, *Intellectual Construction of America*, p. 56.

38. John A. Hostetler, *Amish Society* rev. ed. (Baltimore: Johns Hopkins University Press, 1968).

39. John A. Hawgood, *The Tragedy of German-America* (New York: Putnam's Sons, 1940), pp. 121–23.

40. Ibid., p. 275.

41. Ewa Morawska, *For Bread with Butter: The Life-Worlds of East Central Europeans in Johnstown, Pennsylvania, 1890–1940* (Cambridge: Cambridge University Press, 1985).

42. Ibid., p. 110.

43. Ibid., p. 125.

44. Ibid., pp. 183–85.

45. Ibid., p. 190.

46. Ibid., pp. 171–72.

47. Ibid., pp. 179–80.

48. Cited in ibid., p. 132.

49. Ibid., pp. 244–45.

50. Leonard Dinnerstein and David M. Reimers, *Ethnic Americans: A History of Immigration* (New York: HarperCollins, 1988), p. 60.

51. Cited in ibid., p. 64.

52. Stanford M. Lyman, "Strangers in the City: The Chinese in the Urban Frontier," in Amy Tachiki, Eddie Wong, and Franklin Odo, eds., *Roots: An Asian American Reader* (Los Angeles: UCLA Asian American Studies Center, 1971), pp. 159–87; Victor G. and Brett de Bary Nee, *Longtime Californ': A Document Study of an American Chinatown* (New York: Pantheon Books, 1973), pp. 299–300.

53. David M. Riemers, *Still the Golden Door: The Third World Comes to America* (New York: Columbia University Press, 1992), pp. 104–6.

54. Benjamin Schwartz, *The Thought of Ancient China* (Cambridge: Harvard University Press, 1985), pp. 24, 34; James Legge, *Confucian Analects* (New York: Paragon Book, 1966), pp. 73, 87, 142; Burton Watson, trans., *Hsun Tzu: Basic Writings* (New York: Columbia University Press, 1963), pp. 109–10.

55. Thomas J. Schlereth, *The Cosmopolitan Ideal in Enlightenment Thought* (Notre Dame, Ind.: University of Notre Dame Press, 1977), p. 83.

56. Joseph R. Levenson and Franz Schurmann, *China: An Interpretive History* (Berkeley: University of California Press, 1971), pp. 115–16.

57. Jane Caulton, "D.C. Joins Other School Systems in Push for Afrocentric Reforms," *Washington Times*, August 6, 1990; Joyce Braden Harris, *African and African-American Traditions in Language Arts* (Portland Baseline Essay), p. 30; see Arthur M. Schlesinger Jr., *The Disuniting of America* (Knoxville, Tenn.: Whittle Direct Books, 1991), pp. 31–32.

58. William T. Hagan, *American Indians* (Chicago: University of Chicago Press, 1993), pp. 133–210; Francis Paul Prucha, *The Indians in American So-*

ciety: From the Revolutionary War to the Present (Berkeley: University of California Press, 1985).

59. R. Radhakrishnan makes a similar point, with the help of much heavier intellectual artillery, in "Postmodernism and the Rest of the World," *Organization: Article on Globalization,* 1 (1994), pp. 305–40.

60. Hagan, *American Indians,* p. 203.

61. In American Indian colleges, Indian leaders try to combine modern scientific views with native views in the curriculum. "In an academic course like biology, for example, both the content and way of teaching expand when the Dine [Navajo] Philosophy of Learning is applied. The instructor, while covering everything required in a traditional college biology course, may also teach the Navajo classification systems of plants and animals" (*The American Indian College Fund 1993 Annual Report* [New York: American Indian College Fund], p. 26). The student will need a mind of great power and lucidity to survive such a hybrid course unconfused.

4. Cosmopolite's Viewpoint

1. This is the example used by Ludwig Wittgenstein in his exploration of the meaning of ritual. See Rodney Needham, "Wittgenstein and Ritual," in *Exemplars* (Berkeley: University of California Press, 1985), pp. 163–64.

2. Yi-Fu Tuan, "Community and Place: A Skeptical View," in S. T. Wong, ed., *Person, Place and Thing: Interpretative and Empirical Essays in Cultural Geography,* Geoscience and Man, vol. 31 (Baton Rouge: Department of Geography and Anthropology, Louisiana State University, 1992), pp. 47–59.

3. Martin Buber, *The Writings of Martin Buber* (New York: Meridian Books, 1956), p. 129.

4. M. I. Finley, *The World of Odysseus* (Harmondsworth, Middlesex: Penguin, 1979), p. 64.

5. F. C. Grant, *Ancient Roman Religion* (New York: Liberal Arts Press, 1957), pp. 36–37; Marcel Granet, *Fêtes et chansons anciennes de la Chine* (Paris: Librairie Ernest Leroux, 1929), p. 194; for more references, see Yi-Fu Tuan, "Geopiety: A Theme in Man's Attachment to Nature and to Place," in David Lowenthal and Martyn Bowden, eds., *Geographies of the Mind* (New York: Oxford University Press, 1976), pp. 11–39.

6. David Gilmore, *Aggression and Community: Paradoxes of Andalusian Culture* (New Haven: Yale University Press, 1987).

7. Frederic Cassidy is a linguist at the University of Wisconsin-Madison.

8. Peter Laslett, *The World We Have Lost* (New York: Charles Scribner's, 1971), p. 5.

9. Martha Nussbaum, *The Fragility of Goodness: Luck and Ethics in Greek Tragedy and Philosophy* (Cambridge: Cambridge University Press, 1986), pp. 1–21.

10. Lewis Mumford, *The Myth of the Machine: Technics and Human Development* (New York: Harcourt, Brace & World, 1967).

11. Yi-Fu Tuan, "The City: Its Distance from Nature," *Geographical Review*, 68 (1978), pp. 1–12; on light and speech, see George Steiner, "The Distribution of Discourse," in *On Difficulty and Other Essays* (New York: Oxford University Press, 1978), p. 21, and Ruth Padel, "George Steiner and the Greekness of Tragedy," in Nathan A. Scott Jr. and Ronald A. Sharp, eds., *Reading George Steiner* (Baltimore: Johns Hopkins University Press, 1994), pp. 106–7.

12. Leon Bernard, *The Emerging City: Paris in the Age of Louis XIV* (Durham: Duke University Press, 1970), pp. 162–66.

13. William T. O'Dea, *The Social History of Lighting* (London: Routledge & Kegan Paul, 1958); Mark J. Bouman, "Luxury and Control: The Urbanity of Street Lighting in Nineteenth-Century Cities," *Journal of Urban History*, 14 (1987), pp. 7–37.

14. R. A. E. Hume, *The Thirteen Principal Upanishads* (London: Oxford University Press, 1931), p. 83. On the importance of self-cultivation as distinct from social reform in Confucianism, see W. Theodore de Bary, *The Trouble with Confucianism* (Cambridge: Harvard University Press, 1991), p. 91.

15. Michael Carrithers, *The Buddha* (Oxford: Oxford University Press, 1983), pp. 10–11.

16. Ibid., p. 17.

17. Ibid., p. 84.

18. Kenneth K. S. Ch'en, *Buddhism: The Light of Asia* (Woodbury, N.Y.: Barron's Educational Series, 1968), p. 32; Edward Conze, *Buddhism: Its Essence and Development* (New York: Harper Colophon, 1975), pp. 48–52.

19. J. V. Luce, *An Introduction to Greek Philosophy* (London: Thames & Hudson, 1992), pp. 66–67, 76.

20. Ibid., pp. 81–83.

21. A. E. Taylor, *Socrates: The Man and His Thought* (Garden City, N.Y.: Doubleday Anchor, 1952); Gregory Vlastos, "What Kind of a Man Is He?" in Vlastos, ed., *The Philosophy of Socrates: A Collection of Critical Essays* (New

York: Anchor, 1971), pp. 1–21. Socrates showed his piety—his deference to custom—by wanting to sacrifice a cock to the god of healing, but for what specific favor is not known. An illness in the family? Or was he ironic to the end, thinking that he might induce Asclepius to cure him of the fever of life? See Taylor, *Socrates*, pp. 127–28.

22. Ray Monk, *Ludwig Wittgenstein: The Duty of Genius* (New York: Free Press, 1990), p. 17.

23. On domestic violence in the United States, see Elizabeth Pleck, *Domestic Tyranny: The Making of American Social Policy against Family Violence from Colonial Times to the Present* (New York: Oxford University Press, 1987).

24. Chris Hedges, "Fleeing the Mullah's Men for Hijinks in the Hills," *New York Times*, August 8, 1994, p. 4.

25. Allan Bloom, *Love and Friendship* (New York: Simon & Schuster, 1993), pp. 19, 25, 29–30.

26. Warmth between father and child in classical antiquity is implicit in the following letter addressed by a schoolboy to his father. "It was a fine thing not to take me with you to town! If you won't take me with you to Alexandria, I won't write to you or speak to you or say good-bye to you. If you go to Alexandria, I won't ever take your hand nor greet you again. That is what will happen if you won't take me. Mother said to Archelaus: 'It quite upsets him to be left behind.' It was good of you to send me a present the day you sailed. Send me a lyre, now, I beg you. If you don't, I won't eat, I won't drink. That's that." *Oxyrhyneus Papyri*, CXIX—2nd or 3rd century A.D., trans. from the Greek by F. A. Wright. From Iris Origo, *The Vagabond Path: An Anthology* (London: Chatto & Windus, 1972), p. 104.

27. Victor Lowe, *Alfred North Whitehead: The Man and His Work 1910–1947* (Baltimore: Johns Hopkins University Press, 1990), vol. 2, p. 300.

28. S. L. Washburn and Irven DeVore, "Sexual Behavior of Baboons and Early Man," in Washburn, ed., *Social Life of Early Man* (Chicago: Aldine, 1961), p. 101.

29. Kenneth K. S. Ch'en, *Buddhism in China: A Historical Survey* (Princeton: Princeton University Press, 1964), pp. 263–64; Jacques Gernet, *Daily Life in China on the Eve of the Mongol Invasion 1250–1276* (London: Allen & Unwin, 1962), p. 101.

30. Michael Mollat, *The Poor in the Middle Ages: An Essay in Social History* (New Haven: Yale University Press, 1987); Lewis Mumford, *The City in History* (New York: Harcourt, Brace & World, 1961), pp. 267, 287, 295–96.

31. Merle Curti, *American Philanthropy Abroad: A History* (New Brunswick, N.J.: Rutgers University Press, 1963).

32. Mildred Campbell, *The English Yeoman* (New York: Barnes and Noble, 1960).

33. Lewis Hyde, *The Gift: Imagination and the Erotic Life of Property* (New York: Vintage Books, 1983), pp. 11–24.

34. Yi-Fu Tuan, *Morality and Imagination: Paradoxes of Progress* (Madison: University of Wisconsin Press, 1989), pp. 104–13.

35. Victor Zuckerkandl, *Man the Musician: Sound and Symbol* (Princeton: Bollingen Paperbacks, 1976), pp. 27–30.

36. Glenn Tinder, *Community: Reflections on a Tragic Ideal* (Baton Rouge: Louisiana State University Press, 1980), pp. 30–31.

37. Robert D. Sack, "The Power of Place and Space," *Geographical Review*, 83, (1993), pp. 326–29; J. Nicholas Entrikin, *The Betweenness of Place: Toward a Geography of Modernity* (Baltimore: Johns Hopkins University Press, 1991); J. B. Jackson, *A Sense of Place, a Sense of Time* (New Haven: Yale University Press, 1994).

38. Leszek Kolakowski, *Modernity on Endless Trial* (Chicago: University of Chicago Press, 1990), p. 131.

39. T. S. Eliot, "Little Gidding," *The Complete Poems and Plays 1909–1950* (New York: Harcourt, Brace & World, 1952), p. 145.

40. Boris Pasternak, *Doctor Zhivago* (New York: Ballantine Books, 1981), p. 43.

41. John Carey, *The Intellectuals and the Masses: Pride and Prejudice among the Literary Intelligentsia 1880–1939* (New York: St. Martin's Press, 1992).

42. Steven D. Hoelscher and Robert C. Ostergren, "Old European Homelands in the American Middle West," *Journal of Cultural Geography*, 13 (1993), pp. 87–106; Kathleen N. Conzen, "Ethnicity as Festive Culture: Nineteenth Century German America on Parade," in Werner Sollors, ed., *The Invention of Ethnicity* (New York: Oxford University Press, 1989), pp. 44–76.

43. Scott and Sharp, eds., *Reading George Steiner*, p. 276.

INDEX

YI-FU TUAN was born in China and educated in China (elementary school), Australia (middle school), the Philippines (high school), England (undergraduate school at Oxford), and the United States (graduate school at Berkeley). He was a professor of geography and adjunct professor of American studies at the University of Minnesota before going to the University of Wisconsin-Madison in 1984 as John K. Wright and Vilas Research Professor of Georgraphy. Tuan's books include *Topophilia: A Study of Environmental Perception, Attitudes, and Values* (1974, 1990), *Space and Place: The Perspective of Experience* (Minnesota, 1977), *Landscapes of Fear* (Minnesota, 1979), *Segmented Worlds and Self: Group Life and Individual Consciousness* (Minnesota, 1982), *Dominance and Affection: The Making of Pets* (1984), *The Good Life* (1986), *Morality and Imagination: Paradoxes of Progress* (1989), and *Passing Strange and Wonderful: Aesthetics, Nature, and Culture* (1993).